LOVE LIFE

CATHERINE MCCANN

LOVE

LIFE

A Holistic
Understanding of Ageing

CURRACH
PRESS

First published in 1996 by
Columba Press

This edition, 2018 by
CURRACH PRESS
23 Merrion Square North
Dublin 2, Co. Dublin
www.currach.ie

Cover image and design by Alba Esteban | Currach Press
Printed by Jellyfish Solutions

ISBN 978-1-78218-900-8

Contents

Foreword

It is a pleasure to introduce this helpful and timely book. Catherine McCann was one of the first people in Ireland to recognise the longevity dividend, the extraordinary benefits arising out of our increased lifespan. In addition, her background in healthcare was instrumental in recognising that nurturing and protecting the longevity dividend required significant changes in hearts and minds to move past the fatigued cliché of the failure model of ageing to a more positive and inclusive perspective of our later stages of life.

As later life is marked by increased complexity – we are born copies, but die originals, as we say in gerontology – there is a need for help and guidance in teasing out the ways in which we can age optimally throughout the lifespan. In this book Catherine succeeds admirably in outlining the many factors which can be addressed to empower all of us to continue to flourish in later life. The range of topics covered in an approachable, concise and effective manner is broad, from the practical to the spiritual. She does not shy away from the losses of later life, but provides eminently useful ways to navigate through these areas of concern.

The lifespan perspective is further enhanced though Catherine's own membership of the demographic of later life, an enactment of the theme of 'no more about us without us'. Her inclusion of the spiritual and aesthetic is reflected in her work in developing the calm, tranquil and inspiring sculpture gardens at Shekina, a further major contribution to enriching Irish life. We must all be grateful that Catherine continues to share her wisdom and insights with us with this new book, and in so doing she has made a major contribution to enabling optimal ageing in Ireland.

Professor Desmond (Des) O'Neill
Trinity College Dublin

Preface

Love Life: these two words when combined together name a powerful reality – a reality that sums up what this book is about. *Love Life* came into being as a result of people requesting a republication of a book I wrote on ageing issues over 20 years ago. On rereading that earlier work I noted two realities. Firstly, that many of that book's insights into ageing remained relevant, illustrating that basic human truths remain pertinent despite the sociological changes of the past two decades. Secondly, it also became obvious that certain sections needed updating due to factors such as people living longer; improved knowledge regarding older person's social and health care needs; new technologies appearing (including recent advances in robotics); more accurate research findings.

Hopefully this new book will prove valuable both for those preparing for retirement as well as people who are in these years. The fundamental concept of 'loving life' is captured in each chapter. Ageing is portrayed as a positive process, a time for becoming more and more in love with the unique lifespan we have personally been given and attempting to live this life fully to its completion and, as part of this process, by touching into and being touched by the vibrancy of life that is all around us.

The contents of my previous book emerged from insights gained throughout my physiotherapy career and especially from my final two years prior to retirement when I worked in primary health care and began to realise the importance of the educational aspect of care. An involvement in the plight of family carers followed. This soon broadened to older people's care and to the publication of *Falling in Love with Life* in 1996 just prior to my own retirement later that year when I was 62. That book became the basis of workshops given around most of the counties in Ireland over the following seven years. During retirement, my life and views on life have been enriched by other endeavours such as studying for Master and Doctorate degrees, offering counselling/spiritual direction, travelling to Israel, Ethiopia and India, writing books, caring for a close friend suffering from dementia for eight years, accompanying my brother on his nine-month palliative care journey and working as curator of Shekina Sculpture Garden.

Loving life emerges through adopting appropriate attitudes and behaviours and this comes about through greater understanding. Understanding is more than knowing 'about' things although it can include that. It is knowing something from the 'inside'; a comprehending, a grasping of a truth which causes us to exclaim: 'now I see' or 'I really know what this is about'. Understanding can come in a flash, a moment of truth as we say, but normally it is a process, which over time reveals what is truly real as well as the deeper meanings that lie behind reality. Growth in understanding alters the way we perceive things; it changes the way we think and as a consequence, the way we feel. One of the tragedies of life, according to Anthony de Mello, the Indian mystic, is that there is a shortage of understanding in all of us. He says that often we do not have to do anything to bring about change; it happens through the process of understanding.

Understanding is not just about understanding concepts – it is about understanding our own experiences and desires. It is concerned with the search for meaning, which is an essential activity of the human person. This search often becomes more acute as we age. The wonderings of the child can reappear, but the questions now emerge from a deeper level and from the accumulation of insights gained through our varying life experiences. The world of meanings that we have acquired may require adaptation when facing what lies ahead. A fundamental choice as we age is to add aliveness to our years or, alternatively, to simply add years. Experiencing a sense of aliveness is central to positive ageing.

There are many misconceptions, taboos, myths and fears around ageing. A way to banish or alleviate these is to understand the issues connected to the ageing process. Insight into ageing can enhance enormously the quality of life we live in the present. It also enables us to look more positively at the years that are to come. The secret of living is to live in the present and to live fully each stage of life. Some people's lifespan may be short. Others may live to over a hundred. Quality living, as opposed to a long life without quality, must surely be what is desired.

Having worked with older people – the fragile older person and their families, preparing the 50+ age groups for the years ahead and reflecting on my own 22 years of retirement leads to my want to share with readers the richness as well as the difficulties of this important period in all of our lives. The information in this book provides an opportunity to know more 'about'; it is up to the reader to internalise some of this knowledge and apply it to the changes in attitudes and lifestyle that may be necessary to experience life as fulfilling. Readers may gain new depth into insights already known, others may benefit from realities never thought about before.

Love Life is primarily aimed at those who are 50 or over. When positive and insightful approaches are brought to our future years, life can be not only fulfilling, but fascinating. The approach of this book is holistic. It examines the general happenings that occur as people age, what pitfalls can be avoided and what areas need to be worked at so that we age 'well'.

The first chapter looks at the ageing process in general and the unique phenomena of our time where life expectancy levels have increased enormously. Chapter two is on retirement and the importance of preparing for this time when formal work ends. Chapter three focuses on the importance of a sense of wellbeing and concentrates on what individuals can do, in both practical and psychological ways, to contribute to personal wellbeing. Chapter four explores the question of living positively with disablements, a reality that inevitably occurs. Chapter five discusses the various stresses of this period of life and Chapter six is on its satisfactions. The final chapter reflects on wisdom, the gift par excellence of our mature years, hope, which fosters a sense of optimism and enthusiasm and finally joy with its derivative contentment.

"One only grows old when one loses a sense of adventure." The key adventure of becoming more fully ourselves as we move towards the completion of our lifespan also benefits others – loving life and living it to the full is the best contribution we can offer towards the betterment of humanity.

CHAPTER ONE

The Ageing Process

Experiencing a personal sense of aliveness is what this book is about. We age from the day we are born. Yet when the word ageing is used people assume it refers to the older years. What in fact are the older years? Those who are considered old in one culture will not be in another. Definitions of the older years will also vary among individuals within a culture. Until recently, many considered the older years to begin at the time of retirement which generally meant at 65. A light-hearted answer says that an old person is someone who is 15 years older than we are.

A well-known saying is apt: 'We are as old as we feel'. The experience of most people is that they feel young inside even when certain physical limitations are present. It is important that society in general and each one individually, fosters keeping alive that 'young inside' person.

Only towards the end of life may a change from this outlook become noticeable. The usual manifestation of this is weariness, at both the physical and psychological levels of the person. Such fatigue is often an expression that a person is now tired of living and is readying to leave this life. This phase may be preceded by a period of frailty that moves towards passivity. It is a time when they are unable to be other than this way. A false 'enlightened' view of ageing does not always allow for this period in people's lives. Those around can try to cajole such a person to be and do what they are no longer really able for.

A common way in the western world of looking at ageing is to divide the lifespan into three ages. These divisions are not chronologically or biologically precise but they can act as useful concepts. The first age is from birth to 18 years. This is a time for development. The second age is from 18 to 60 years. This period is for formal work and child rearing. From the sixties onwards these tasks are largely over or nearing completion. The question then is what is this period of life for? I suggest it is a time for fulfilment, a time of opportunity to enrich one's life in a broad spectrum of ways (ways that will be discussed further in the chapter on retirement).

The above three divisions are today changing somewhat. For example, due to extended periods of education, some to doctorate level, or prolonged periods of training for a career, work may only commence in the 20-25 age bracket. The period of child rearing is also beginning at a later stage leading to parenting continuing until the early sixties.

From the Bronze Age (around 2500 BC) until the mid-19th century, a period of 4,500 years, life expectancy rose from 18 to 36 years. From the mid-19th century until now, in other words a period of around 200 years, that figure has doubled. At present, life expectancy in the western world is into the mid-eighties. Many obvious factors have led to this: improved sanitation, nutrition, housing, education and discoveries of all kinds, the most recent including the huge modern technological and pharmacological advances. The one great achievement that has caused life expectancy levels to rise has been the dramatic drop in infant mortality. Death in modern society is now largely due to old age. This does not mean that individual members of the race are living longer. People in previous ages of history have lived to over a hundred. The difference now is that more people are surviving into their older years. The number living over 70 has trebled in recent years.

The fact that so many are living into their eighties, nineties, and a hundred plus is surely a great achievement, a great victory for humanity. However not everyone sees this as an achievement. Some view it as a problem. Over the period of a century we see the average life expectancy for women today has reached 86 and is set to arise in forty years' time to 90, and for men it is presently 83 and rising in a similar time frame to 87. This lengthening of lifespan is hugely dramatic - in 1917 it was a mere 50 years for women and 45 for men. The statistics from the recent 2016 census show 30% of the Irish population are over

50; 18.4% are over 60; 5.8% are over 70; 2.8% are over 80 and 0.4% are in the 90+ years.

Problems will undoubtedly exist if nations and individuals do not take cognisance of, and plan for, this reality. Planning is required in many different areas such as good pensions schemes, health and social care systems, suitable housing (houses should be designed for the needs of both young and older people), educational programmes that prepare for and allow for fulfilled living in these years. These realities should be considered the norm for the vast majority of people.

The fact that a greater number of people survive inevitably makes huge changes in society. It can change consumer power, for example advertising. The arrangements of supermarket shelves are now geared towards older people's needs. The greater number of frail older persons will mean more people leaning on a State's limited resources. Some are fearful that this need will happen at the expense of other groups who also require care services.

Ethical questions such as euthanasia, or its opposite, prolonging life by complicated means with high expenditure involved, are becoming pressing issues. Many complex and difficult problems are already occurring and need to be faced by societies and their politicians. Overall government and other groups in society need to provide a suitable environment, in the general meaning of this word, for people to grow old into. Planners must see that preventative measures are in place for health, social and financial care, as well as providing adequate and appropriate housing, leisure and other facilities. Older people themselves should be included in the formation of all policies related to their care.

More recently, there is a movement towards dependant older people with varying types of illnesses and disabilities remaining on in their home. This necessitates being able to receive appropriate carer services, as well as adaptations to the house should these be necessary. Homes in future should be built with facilities that cater for the needs of all age groups. Ideally, requirements like suitable access, including doors wide enough for wheelchairs, and a downstairs bathroom should be considered before homes are built, namely at the planning stage. Nursing homes are necessary for those with complicated medical care needs, for those with severe dementia, or where two carers at a time are needed to safely move a person.

The EU selected five priority areas in relation to older people: the role and potential of the active retired; improving the situation of older women; management of an older workforce; transition from work to retirement, access to care for dependant older people. Their overall orientation is seeing older persons as a resource and not a burden, and to implement this fact in all policies related to older people.

Education is the key factor in improving facilities for older people. Education of politicians and professionals, as well as the general public, is required so that everyone can face the situation of people living longer constructively and optimistically. Education has both a negative and positive role – negative in the sense of eliminating myths in regard to ageing, and positive in opening up possibilities so that fulfilled ageing becomes a reality for the majority of people.

The fact that, in the first quarter of this century, far more people are living into their nineties or beyond should be celebrated. However, a question requires attention: is this extension of life to continue? There are signs of a downward trend in some western world countries. In Ireland today, social inequality, an extreme shortage of housing, drug, alcohol and obesity problems will all manifest their negative effects in years to come, one being a shortening of lifespan.

While most are adapting to people living longer, ageism is still a reality. Like other 'isms' its removal takes time and action such as the rooting out of attitudes and changing of structures and laws that buttress its continuation. Attitudes towards ageing develop from various sources but come particularly from our personal experiences with older people and from experiences we have had with close older relatives. If that experience was negative it can affect us for the rest of our lives. Research has shown that definite attitudes, positive or negative can begin as early as eight years of age. Older people can be victimised in many ways by ageist attitudes and they themselves can perpetuate the problem by unknowingly participating and continuing in false roles and behaviours that colour all aspects of living. Misconceptions can include equating the older years with sickness. Old age is not a pathological state. People can become ill when old as they do other age groups. True, older people tend to have more than one complaint but many of these are likely to be chronic conditions. These can be managed, but the person is not ill because they are left with certain limitation of functioning. Small children cannot carry out all tasks for themselves, hence they are dependent on others, but we do not consider them ill as a result.

Misconceptions also occur around expectations as shown by the following examples. People sometimes expect older people to have certain antiquated values and ideas and can be surprised when they hear their actual views, which may be far more progressive than their own. It is assumed that older people are expected to do or not do certain things, or to behave according to a preconceived stereotype. For example, some do not expect older people to be sexually active. This misconception is particularly true among middle-aged children of older parents. Prejudices and negative stereotyping of all kinds need to be challenged. A patient takes on such a challenge when going to the doctor with a painful knee. The doctor remarks: 'What can you expect at your age?' to which the patient replies, 'The other knee is just as old and is quite healthy!'

On the more positive side, education needs to promote personal responsibility for adopting a healthy lifestyle and how to manage financial affairs realistically. Planning for adequate pension, insurance and other saving schemes needs to be introduced early in life and be evaluated throughout the middle years. It is never too early to start working on these issues, but it can often be too late, making finance a major problem in our older years. Alas, the shortage of housing in present day Ireland has led to people coming later to starting a mortgage and often at such a high rate that pensions and savings take second place.

People sometimes ask what they can do to help older people. The best contribution anyone can make is to care for ourselves in the present in an educated way, and thus prevent or lessen the likelihood of becoming a problem for others when we in turn are old. A large part of all education is to normalise the ageing process, by neither denying it nor allowing it become a disempowering stage in life. It is essential healthy attitudes are promoted. The most fundamental attitude is to approach ageing as something we create ourselves rather than view it as a passively given reality. In other words, we 'make' our own older years to a great extent. It is a period when we need to work at making things happen, as well as allowing for and accepting those happenings over which we have no control. Approaching our older years in a positive manner greatly lessens the possibility of apathy and depression taking hold. Depression can become a major factor for some and this can remain hidden. It is said by some experts to be a greater problem than dementia. Only 5% of the population over 65 suffers from dementia, although that figure does rise with age to 20% for the over eighties. It is still only a small proportion of the older population. We have only a minimal say in preventing dementia, but we can help in preventing or lessening the effects of depression. Some older people have severe depressive disorders, others have milder forms. In addition, some develop anxieties or phobias. Both can be helped by counselling or medication or a combination of both.

There are certain established criteria for ageing well. These include good morale, self-esteem, experiencing satisfaction in our ordinary everyday living, having control over our lives. Erikson, the great American psychoanalyst, speaks of certain features in later life which help to make the above experiences possible. The abilities we need to develop are the following: to be able to adapt to change, to accept the past, to transcend self-preoccupation, and to lose a fear of death. People will come in their own way to degrees of achievement of some or all of these.

※ A major ability or quality that everyone needs in life and especially in the older years is adaptability; to be able to adjust to the inevitable biological, spiritual and social changes that ageing brings. Acceptance of things that cannot be changed is part of this adjustment. Coming to acceptance of what is limiting and undesirable involves discovering meaning in what has taken place. Over time this meaning can deepen.

※ The ability to accept our past life. This includes reconciling how we have actually lived our lives and how we might like to have lived them. Acceptance of mistakes or, choices made that are now regretted, helps to contribute to present levels of satisfaction. An inability to do this will detract from an experience of wellbeing.

※ Transcendence of self-preoccupation is difficult; it is part of everyone's lifelong fight against selfishness. It is sad to see older people whose lives centre more and more on themselves and their needs, with a gradual decline of interest and awareness of the needs of others. This can happen to people who may have been very caring earlier in life.

※ Attitudes towards death have been neglected in many studies on ageing. This could be the result of researchers showing a conscious or unconscious fear or uneasiness about their own mortality, or it could be out of respect for such a sacred moment in life. Fear is an emotion related to the unknown and death is the great unknown for all of us. Some people have a great fear of death. Others face it calmly, and those who work in hospitals would say that the latter is true of most people. Religion can play a part in helping people cope with death and dying, yet some, despite their deep faith, can have a great natural fear of death. The actual reality of death grows in people's consciousness from the seventies onwards when an awareness of our own mortality impinges more into living. This can lead to moroseness, but for those with a healthy realism it can lead to a greater appreciation of the preciousness of life. This in turn results in a determination to try and live as fully as possible each new decade, each new year, each new day, as they come along.

There is a theory that many people develop *efficiency* at the cost of *versatility*. The patterns of thinking and behaviour that we adopt, particularly over the middle years, tend to colour our later lives. A lack of versatility shows itself in an inability to try out new things, take risks, even to enlarge interest and ways of thinking about things. This can result in people being only able to make restrictive choices in their later years when in fact this is a time when creativity is needed. Flexibility and a resourceful spirit are great qualities to bring into the older years. When these are diminished, even small changes can be difficult, like changing personal routines or ways of doing things. If more major changes are deemed necessary, these can become catastrophes.

Developing our potential, and being realistically prepared for what lies ahead, are great assets in dealing with the variety of demands that ageing brings. Part of being prepared is holding in awareness a sense of balance of what the future could hold. The good news is that about 80% of older people remain active and independent until near the end of their lives. 15% will require help at home in the form of a carer and the oversight of professionals, while 5% will need nursing home care. We are therefore likely to be in the 80% group. However, we could find ourselves in the other 20% and it is good, at least at times, to allow ourselves look at this possibility. The benefits of this are twofold. Firstly, it can motivate us to do what we can to prevent such a happening. Secondly, it can make it just that bit easier to accept and live positively with this reality should it occur, by the very fact of not being totally unprepared. Examples of limitations could include the following: physical limitations leading to the need for extra support which causes lack of independence and where support is required; financial limitation that necessitates giving up an accustomed lifestyle; the necessity to receive care at home or ultimately nursing home care; and, most painful of all, the loss of normal mental functioning through dementia.

One effect of developing our potential is that we become more differentiated or individual as we age, due to the cumulative effect of personal life experiences. A group of teenagers will be much more like each other, due to the lack of variety in their experience. Because of an older person's greater uniqueness, it is important that we remain our own kind of person and engage in tasks that have value for us, no matter how strange or eccentric our behaviour may appear to others. Florida Maxwell, an American writer, has these striking words to say about herself: "Age puzzles me. I thought it was a quiet time. My seventies were interesting and fairly serene but my eighties are passionate. I grow more intense as I age. To my own surprise I burst out with hot conviction." Our older years call for boldness and imagination. Hence it is important to be wary of telling people how to behave by prescribing how they should live their lives. Widening horizons and encouraging a daring spirit is what needs to be fostered.

Having said this, one thing is definite: the most vital element in ageing well is to keep a sense of purpose to life and one could add a sense of humour. To have a purpose for our older years in general, and to have a goal or goals for each year, even months ahead, is essential to fulfilled living. In practice this means having a sense of purpose as each new day begins. It means not constantly giving into our inner voice which could say something like,

'Stay on in bed today, the weather is too bad'. Awareness of purpose may grow dim and narrow at times due to illness or stress, but fanning it into flame again and again so that it is personally real in the nitty-gritty of everyday happenings is what gives energy and meaning to living life fully to its completion.

CHAPTER TWO

Retirement

Retirement is a strange term and is not really apt to describe the period of life it refers to. The word itself speaks of a movement away from something but gives no indication of where that movement is going. It is this lack of direction that makes the term unhelpful. It clearly shows it is an end of something but it is less obvious that it is about the beginning of something else.

Retirement for many people is a major life event. In many cases it involves a transition from one status in society to a status which is less clear and which often has an 'ex' note about it. For instance, we speak of an ex-nurse, ex-postman, ex-politician. It insinuates a withdrawal into a life without purpose. Retirement can be viewed in a negative and narrow way and, as a result, as uninviting. For most people retirement is understood as that period of life when formal paid work ends.

Yet this view is somewhat narrow as well as changing. Three decades ago most men retired at 65 and died about seven years later. Now several choose to retire at 60, or even earlier and live to their late eighties, almost 30 years later. Continuing improvement in health care, the greater availability of a wide range of educational opportunities and better-informed lifestyles have all helped increased lifespan.

For most people a definite change takes place when the responsibility of child rearing and work come to an end. This change may be painful for some and especially those who perceive it in terms of loss such as: loss of status, routine, money, sense of purpose in life with the possibilities of a life-changing illness, lack of mobility and independence kept in the foreground. For others it is something warmly welcomed. It is likely to be more difficult for those who have been 'workaholics'; who have experienced their self-worth as attached to their role. Parents who find it hard to let go of their children as they grow into adulthood can also find a changing role difficult. Those who look forward to retirement are likely to be persons who have a broad view of life, have a range of interests, and can look ahead with pleasure to their older years as a time of opportunity.

Retirement has certain characteristics. Certainly life becomes less formally structured and the structures that do exist are likely to be those chosen by ourselves. Some find the transition from an ordered existence a relief, whereas others are uncomfortable when they have to move out of a regular timetable that they may have been accustomed to for years. Alan Omstead, an American journalist, wrote an insightful diary following his retirement. He discovered that nothing really out there depended on him. Nothing was imposed; there was nothing he really had to do. He spoke of the cancer-like idea which tempts and says 'do nothing'. He said a deliberate act of will was needed to escape such thoughts and that, without externally-imposed demands on time, there is a need for self-imposed demands. He saw clearly that most activities make a difference for oneself. He also made the interesting remark that self-imposed routines create the possibility for leisure: "They are the bread and butter of the leisure sandwich. Leisure, freedom from obligations, can only exist in relation to obligations." Another commentator, Rachel Walker remarks on "The fact that we are living longer is both the greatest triumph – and the greatest challenge - of the 21st century." She refers to "the blessings of ageing" but also remarks on a negative factor that "our world glorifies the preservation of a youthful appearance over the face that accompanies old age". In summary, it is clear that both positive and negative viewpoints on ageing abound; the aim of this book is to stress a sense of realism coupled with a positive perspective.

Some people look forward to retirement, to engaging more fully in various projects and activities they did not previously have time for. Yet when they actually retire they never get down to what they intended to do. Some find they have time on their hands and yet do not have the will, or discipline, to make these aspirations a reality in their lives. The early retirement years in particular have a lot to do with making things happen rather than just letting them happen.

Retirement alters many areas in our lives, for example, relationships, financial status, responsibilities, the use of time, diminishing energy levels. The changes that occur can intimately affect the way we experience life for the remainder of our years. For some this can be an empowering happening, for others disempowering. It can be disempowering if individuals experience themselves as: 'I am who I was'. It is up to each one of us to choose. Consequent on this basic choice are the multiple choices open to us when we are retired. The range of options is so varied that some find that very fact stressful. Surveys show that our ability and willingness to exercise choice depends on a number of factors, such as education, health, social status, self-esteem, as well as the opportunities we have had to do so in previous years. It is a time for relinquishing the many 'shoulds' and 'oughts' that we previously found ourselves tied by. Part of the transition in retirement is discovering that this is mainly a time for what we want to do and is not about what we feel we ought to be doing.

The pre-retirement years

While this section is concerned with the five to ten years that precede retirement there should, ideally, at the commencement of work, be some thought and action given to the question of pensions. Alas other financial commitments/priorities, thoughtlessness, or an inability to look ahead, make such a happening a rare event. Hopefully by the early thirties some form of pension or savings plan is in place. If a choice had to be made between pension or savings, pension seems a more desirable option as it offers some tax benefit. These arrangements require reviewing throughout one's working life. The quality of our retirement depends to an extent on having adequate finances to cover these important years. In general people's financial literacy levels are low. A module on finance should be included in the curriculum towards the end of secondary school.

Ageing became the topic of Ireland's 'Citizen's Assembly' in Spring 2017. Its focus was primarily on the State's pension scheme. State pensions began in Ireland in 1909 for people over 70. Over many decades since, eligibility for this pension has remained at 66 despite the fact that people are living considerably longer and at better health levels. In the light of these facts and other social changes, it seems desirable and reasonable that over the next three decades this date should progressively move towards 70, namely to where it started. The pension is set to rise from 66 to 67 in 2021 and to 68 in 2028. Exceptions might be necessary for some working groups where possibly a health assessment might be needed if earlier retirement from a health perspective is deemed necessary. For the general worker the length of one's working life will remain unaltered since work is frequently starting five years later due to additional education and training programmes becoming a necessary norm.

A recent major difficulty has arisen in relation to the commencement of supplementary pension schemes or saving plans due to extremely high rent and mortgage rates. This critical factor has forced people to start buying a home at an older age than in previous decades. There is in addition the negative reality that technological advances are leading towards less jobs becoming available in the labour market. The answers to these dilemmas are truly difficult.

People's experiences of their pre-retirement years will differ. For some, the last few years might be difficult and this could negatively affect their approach to retirement. A reason could be an over-valuation of younger workers coupled with an undervaluation of the older worker's contribution. Feeling undervalued can easily lead towards pessimism. In addition, fears of illness, a sense of dependency, plus, perhaps despondency when, for example, seeing one's changing physical appearance, can all have a psychological impact which could lead towards feelings of diminishment. Others may have had good experiences in their last decade at work. Some may have remained on 'top' at what they were doing, while others may decide not to take on extra responsibilities, or, for instance, reduce their working hours as retirement approaches. Whatever approach is taken in those final working years, the importance of remaining very much alive is paramount. Part of one's energy should be geared towards looking ahead towards future possibilities and even trying out new activities in small ways in non-working hours.

There are often varied routes into retirement that enable the boundaries between full work and complete retirement to become blurred. The transition into retirement for non-public sector workers is more flexible, some taking early retirement while others continue on after 65. For some early retirement schemes, voluntary redundancies and more versatile pension arrangements make leaving the workforce more palatable. The self-employed and those working in the private sector are more likely to have alternative options of easing themselves into retirement. In the past the main reason for early retirement was ill health. Now it is can be labour-market related, or, alternatively it can be the worker's choice to move towards other pursuits. These could include furthering one's education, travel, volunteering, other forms of part time work or leisure activities. These realities can be valued and seen as important enough to entice some people from work earlier than anticipated. The timing and meaning of retirement is not always open to personal choice. Regardless of the when and how, it is good to realise that our pleasant or unpleasant anticipation of the retirement years affects not only retirement itself but also quality of life in the years that precede it.

Preparing for Retirement

Understanding ageing and the many issues related to it is the best overall way to prepare for retirement. Some people avoid all preparation because it would seem they do not want to think about it. This group mainly comprises those whose almost sole interest in life has been their work. Research has shown that these people die at an earlier age than the norm.

Retirement is just as important a stage in life as previous ones. Lengthwise it can comprise over a third of our lifespan. It needs to be perceived not merely as a period of 'not working' but a time full of possibilities, including that of remaining or contributing even more to the good of society. It provides an opportunity to make a fresh start – a start which flows from the wealth of our previous life experiences. It turns out for some that they were never as busy as they are now since retiring. Such people experience retirement as giving a new lease of life. For those who do not move through the work to retirement phase of life, namely the unemployed and others, there is a danger of drifting into the older years. Such people are denied the 'fresh start' opportunity which retirement offers. Thought, planning and educational programmes to prepare for the older years are, it could be argued forcibly, just as important for such people.

Preparation for retirement calls for reflection on the meaning of the years that lie ahead and on the particular activities best suited to realising that meaning. The process of reflection prevents us sliding into apathy, to a way of life where existing rather than fulfilling becomes the norm. There is so much potential in all of us that we have never used. We all have talents and insights which were under-utilised or were not utilised at all. Our older years provide the opportunity to redress this. Courage, an ability to take risks, knowing how to manage failure in a positive way, are all helpful attributes that enable us to launch into the deep of new adventures.

While working on attitudes and approaches towards retirement is the basic preparation, looking at practical issues is also necessary. Many people would do this in a personal way, but some form of help can prove beneficial. Some employers offer pre-retirement courses and, if one of these is not available, being adequately informed on financial matters, including entitlements, legal, health, safety and other issues, can prove valuable. The challenge, too, of being opened to the range of facilities and opportunities available, some of which were likely to have been previously unknown, can also be beneficial. The words of the fool to the king in Shakespeare's *King Lear* are apt: "We should not grow older before we grow wiser." Preparation is all about seeking the necessary wisdom before embarking on retirement. This helps us avoid unnecessary pitfalls and, more positively, opens us to a wealth of opportunities.

Financial issues, while already touched on in relation to pensions, require further thought. Adequate financial security relieves what could be a worry and makes for our older years being comfortable and pleasing. Finance is necessary for so many things such as embarking on certain projects/activities of all kinds including travel. The level of optimism we have when viewing our future is often linked to our level of financial security. Financial fears are common and can be real or imagined. Income in old age can come from four sources – state pensions, occupational pensions, savings or part-time work. Those who are fortunate may have two or more of these sources to draw on. Whatever form of 'nest-egg' has been accrued, a reduction in income is certain when we retire. This may lead to the need to adjust our lifestyle. Someone who is unprepared to face the reality of what a drop in income entails is likely to fare less well than the person who has thought through such implications. Professional help may be necessary if the income drop is severe. Unnecessary fears can make us tight with money, leading to an inability to enjoy a lifestyle that is affordable.

Ideally people should start to save younger. This is extremely difficult for many and even for those who can. Looking ahead to the older years is not seen as a priority for 20 and 30-year-olds, or even for those in their forties who only recently have acquired a mortgage or started having a family. A unique phenomenon in Ireland is the number of people who own, or desire to own their own home. While this is desirable in many respects, it does leave people with less fluid assets available in their older years. A question to be faced is whether home ownership is the best way to sustain quality living in our older years, or should alternatives be considered?

The Retirement Years

Retirement can be a fruitful and enjoyable time. To assist this occurrence five topics are given special attention: relationships and roles, leisure, education/development, volunteering and creativity including exposure to the arts.

1. *Relationships/Roles*

Major life changes, of which retirement is certainly one, affects other aspects of our lives and the key one is our relationships. The chief sustaining factor throughout life is healthy relationships and the alterations that retirement brings can have beneficial or adverse effects. Awareness of this is very important for fulfilment in the older years. The more crucial relationships are examined below, particularly in relation to possible problem areas.

a) Partnership relationships

Partnership relationships can flourish in new ways in the older years. Some may run into difficulties. A common scenario is the following. A husband, wife or partner whose main focus in life up to retirement has been their job/career may have devoted much of their energy, interest and time in this direction with the result that little quality time was available for their togetherness; family life in general. Such a person may have largely postponed the notion of family satisfaction until their later years.

When retirement arrives they could discover they have missed moments which can never be recaptured and may have to grapple with the realisation that their children have grown away from them, either physically or psychologically or both. The other partner, due to this absence in home matters and often poor quality presence when they are around, are liable to have made a life of their own, where their interests and needs are met by friendships and activities in which the other partner is not involved. In other words, both partners have grown apart from each other in core aspects of each other's lives. It will take time and work for a satisfying relationship to develop again, especially in the altered situation where children may no longer be around. The predominant 'home-maker' partner may resent their partner coming back to the household full-time, intruding in what has over the years become more and more 'their domain'. Retirement for one can mean an intrusion in the lifestyle developed by the other. Tensions will almost inevitably surface between the couple. Feelings such as resentment and disillusionment could easily emerge.

With children no longer the focus of their main shared interest, it takes understanding of where the other has come from and determination to work afresh at their couple relationship. Coming unstuck from patterns of living that have grown up over time is never easy, hence it is imperative that an effort be made by both if a fulfilled existence for the remainder of their years is the desired aim. Sensitive adjustment that allows for individual freedom as well as togetherness has to be worked out in a way that is acceptable for both. Many discover that this is a completely new period in their life as a partnership, a time when their togetherness can flourish in new and exciting ways.

b) Children/sibling/friendship/community relationships

All these sets of relationships can grow or become under strain at the time of retirement. This is particularly the case when such persons share the same home. Adjustment is called for on all sides. Allowing each other freedom and being prepared to alter expectations of one another in matters like altered routines can be helpful. Generosity and avoidance of demanding behaviour is called for by all involved.

In early retirement it can be helpful to review inheritance plans. Family rows and splits can occur if there is lack of clarity around this issue. It is particularly important for those in partner relationships who have children that they have full civil law protection. Some adult children can subtly or directly show an assumed right to claim some of their parent's wealth, be it property, or capital. Parents may need to exercise their right to hold onto what is theirs for their own quality living and not be persuaded to feel badly doing this unless there is a good reason to the contrary. If for example in later years nursing homecare is deemed appropriate, the present Fair Deal system will be activated and issues around the family home will arise in relation to payment of such care.

Existing friendship relationships should be cherished and fostered. To be open to the opportunity to make new friends as one's new lifestyle falls into place is important, as work friends may recede and the death of some friends can lead to one's familiar circle of friends shrinking.

As patterns of future behaviour are being laid down in the early retirement years, thought should be given to our later years from a variety of perspectives. An important reality is to look at the benefits that accrue from developing positive community relationships. When a partner dies and children move away, possibly to foreign countries, the need for local supportive relationships could prove invaluable. Later retirement years can lead to social isolation and its by-product, loneliness. Community support can come in many ways, local gatherings and different forms of activities being one, with conversation maybe proving the most valuable benefit of all. Good community support could offer another important reality, namely, by providing the additional support that might be necessary to allow a person remain in their own home as their health declines. Recent research is showing that social interaction plays a key role in successful ageing.

c) Grandchildren

Relationships with grandchildren and the question of the grand-parenting role can take on great significance following retirement. This is an important but sensitive area that requires delicate handling. Grandchildren and great-grandchildren can be one of the delights of the older years, provided healthy relationships are established between grandparents, children and grandchildren. There are pitfalls. For example, adult children can ask their parents to look after their children, possibly to give them an occupation following retirement and more likely to allow themselves to continue working with greater ease. Such a situation can start off as beneficial to all concerned but can go awry unless constant reevaluation is allowed for.

Grandparents can take on the role willingly to start with, but may find later the demands and the energy drain too high. They may also come to feel taken for granted by their children and begin to resent being so tied down. Early on or later in their grandchildren-minding role, they can come to realise that other opportunities are being lost, that there are other avenues in life they would like to have followed and maybe now it is too late to do so. They may feel uncomfortable about going back on the commitment they gave to their child. If only one grandparent is involved, it can become a source of tension between the grandparents or it could cut across the grandparents having more time together for rebuilding afresh their own relationship.

The actual minding of children's children can be fraught, when ideologies and standards about child rearing differ between grandparents and parents. Some grandparents might be seen as too indulgent, others as too strict. Finding a balance that is helpful and does not confuse the child is particularly necessary. Having pointed out some pitfalls, there is a need to re-emphasise that healthy fostering of relationships between grandparents and grandchildren can be a source of great delight and of enormous benefit to both parties. A recent British report estimated that grandparents delivered £7.3bn worth of care annually! Savings are likely to be proportionally similar in Ireland today.

2. *Leisure*

Leisure is something different from free time. Free time is sometimes termed 'non-obligated' time when seen in relation to work. Leisure is a particular use of non-obligated time. The importance of personal choice is vital in the activities an individual selects. The number of leisure pursuits is endless and, obviously, what is leisure for one may not be for another. The essential note in leisure is that it is something we enjoy. A leisure pursuit has the added dimension of having some discipline attached. For instance, if swimming is chosen as a leisure pursuit then we go regularly, even on the odd day we do not particularly feel like doing so. If some discipline is not present, whatever the pursuit is, the activity is likely to peter out over a short period of time. A real problem that occurs for some people is that they have had, or made opportunity for, little leisure time during their working life and so are poorly prepared to make good use of their free time when retired.

Leisure activities include all forms of sport, such as golf, bowling, darts, plus for some the more active sports like running, cycling, tennis as well as yoga, keep-fit and Pilates. A daily walk ranks high on positive ageing research findings. Other leisure activities could include card games, chess, reading clubs, different forms of community gatherings and outings, men's sheds, working in allotments, theatre, cinema and dancing. More personal forms of leisure could include activities like reading, doing crosswords, listening to music, going to concerts, visiting galleries or other hobbies.

A significant leisure event is travel. Travel can vary from a few days to several months, either abroad or in Ireland. Due to lowering of airfares, anywhere in the world is possible, finance being the main limitation. Those with certain health limitations have recently benefited from the expansion of cruise holidays.

What can prevent some people from participating in outside-the-home leisure pursuits is lack of adequate transport, as well as suitable premises and facilities. Providers of all forms of leisure activities need to take greater account of the problems of some older people.

3. *Education and personal development*

A remarkable feature in the past two decades is the number of people who return to education in their retirement years. Courses are available on a wide range of topics. Some choose studies in fields they have never explored; others study topics they know but they want to follow their hunger for further knowledge and possibly at a higher level. People of today are working for a Masters or Doctorate in their seventies. The range of possible topics is vast. The diversity of interests is well catered for in most universities and colleges as well as online. Starting to study again may be daunting to start with but the challenge involved can prove extremely worthwhile as I discovered myself. The week I retired, I started on a Masters and eight years later embarked on a Doctorate. A particular advantage in further studies is the mixing with other students, both young and old, a factor which is likely to prove stimulating.

The University of the Third Age (U3A) deserves special mention. Such groups were promoted in Ireland by Age Action 20 years ago. There are now about 30 groups around the country and growing. Age Action is willing to help in the setting up of new U3A groups. A big positive for some people is that no qualifications are needed to join. Learning computer skills has been popular. Topics can range from the intellectual to the practical depending on the group. The social dimension of joining U3A, includes enlivening conversations. The latter can turn out to be as beneficial as the learning itself.

More is said about the advantage of further education in the following chapter under the subtitle 'Intellectual Wellbeing'.

4. *Creativity*

A great sign of vitality in life is creativity. The middle years for many have been a functional period of life, where working to build a home, rear a family and attend to work, are uppermost values, and towards these most personal energy was directed. Our older years are, as previously suggested, a time for fulfilment. It is a time par excellence for unleashing the creative self which may have been stunted to the point where individuals say they have no creativity. This is never true. The way we do things, for instance, set a table, the way we dress, the gestures we make with our face, hands, body, are all creative actions.

One of the great joys in retirement is to enlarge the creative part of us that lies deep within. It may be discovered in specific art forms such as painting, sculpture, poetry, drama, dance, writing, composing, performance art, crafts; or it may disclose itself in more hidden ways of thought, ways of relating to others or the world; or in meditation/prayer. Creativity can come through the appreciation of many art forms as well as participating in the art itself. More will be explored on this topic in the chapter on the satisfaction of the older years.

5. *Volunteering/service to others*

Discovering a meaningful role in society after retirement is often achieved through voluntary work. Such work can be of a formal or informal nature. The former normally entails joining an organisation, club or society. The range of possibilities is vast; for example, they could be connected with politics, civil life in general, the arts, sport, religion or social issues. Active Retirement organisations, most of them being geographically based, can also open up people to a great variety of activities and projects within one's own locality. Helping out at local churches or clubs are examples of less formal voluntary work. Informal volunteering, or acts of service of all kinds, is something people opt for as individuals. A few people may join together on some project and form a small informal group.

An essential note to quality living is to know that we are still contributing to society, to know that we are givers as well as receivers in our relationships with others. The actual level of contribution may be small, but if it is meaningful that is what makes the difference. Volunteering, or acts of service, enhance self-worth and contribute a great deal to the realisation that life is worthwhile. To be able to go on giving to people, or to projects that benefit others, keeps alive a sense of purpose to living. Skills, talents, insights and the other riches developed over life can be beneficial to others, often in unexpected ways and unusual circumstances. Having confidence in the value of our contribution is also helpful for oneself. The mutuality of the help that is given and the help that is received can assist in restoring a present imbalance where the 'wisdom of the expert' is seen to outshine the 'wisdom of the years'. Both forms of wisdom call for respect and both in their own way have something special to contribute to enriching the lives of others.

Some choose to use their well-honed skills, professional or other, in less developed countries following retirement. Indeed the scope for volunteering work is endless. Looking at websites such as *volunteering.ie* could prove helpful. It can be beneficial to ponder on the wide range of possibilities that are available some years before retirement commences.

Keeping in touch with current affairs, both local and worldwide, through newspapers, periodicals or television can expand our vision. A danger to avoid is letting our worldview shrink due to our focus becoming overly centred on oneself.

CHAPTER THREE

A sense of wellbeing

A sense of wellbeing is an important part of experiencing life as fulfilling. Wellbeing is the result of reasonably met personal needs. We all have physical, intellectual, emotional and spiritual needs which require attention. All four need to be met in a balanced way if a sense of wellbeing is to be achieved. Some people, for example, care well for physical needs but may fall short in some of the other areas. We tend to be preoccupied with some needs more than others because of personal interests and circumstances.

However, it is necessary that thought and time be given to attending to all four areas, which make up what it is to be a fully human person. For example, we cannot become truly integrated if we live solely from the head or at the level of feelings, if we over 'spiritualise' all aspects of living, or become too body-centred. In other words, when there is an over-concentration of energy on one, two or even three areas at the expense of the fourth, wellbeing and fulfilment will be diminished in some way.

Success depends on taking responsibility for the care of our own physical and mental health. In our earlier years, conscious thought about such matters is likely to have been scanty or spasmodic. From the fifties on, it becomes more important to think through issues related to physical, intellectual, emotional and spiritual wellbeing. This needs to be done, not merely in a reactive way in response to problems that arise, but in a pro-active manner, so that difficulties are prevented or their effects lessened in severity.

Appropriate lifestyles cannot be imposed on anyone; they are the result of personal choices. These choices are influenced by knowledge and an understanding of the values that make for wellbeing. Some people have the impression that healthy living is a negative concept; where multiple restrictions dominate our lives. On the contrary, a sense of wellbeing is about joy, humour, even exuberance, coupled with the discipline of moderation and knowing how to balance the different areas of living.

Physical wellbeing

Physical wellbeing is greatly influenced by our relationship to our own bodies. Many people have difficulty accepting, let alone liking and appreciating their bodies. Some are often not comfortable with their size, shape, particular features, or certain functional abilities. This can start in adolescence or earlier and is not helped by advertising and a general ethos in society which portrays attractiveness in terms of a certain kind of beauty which is related to youthfulness, slimness, agility and 'good looks'. Yet each human body in its uniqueness is attractive in its own way. We all have a responsibility not to 'spoil' this unnecessarily through unhealthy behaviour or lack of personal care, but to enhance it through adequate and appropriate exercise, rest, diet, and attention to personal appearance.

As people age, the body will consciously claim more attention. It is far easier to give this attention with kindness and care if we are comfortable with, respect and even appreciate our ageing and less efficient body. It is easier to cope with the possible annoyances that certain limitations may bring if we have learnt to befriend our body throughout life.

The following linear diagram illustrates that health and wellbeing are much more than an absence of sickness. The numbers in the diagram do not refer to years, but are figures which indicate levels of wellness. At number 50 on the line, all that can be said is that we have no symptoms of illness. Although this particular section deals with physical wellbeing, mental health levels are also included in this illustration.

Health wellness levels

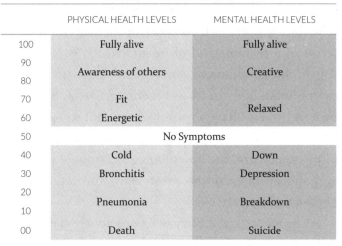

	PHYSICAL HEALTH LEVELS	MENTAL HEALTH LEVELS
100	Fully alive	Fully alive
90	Awareness of others	Creative
80		
70	Fit	Relaxed
60	Energetic	
50	No Symptoms	
40	Cold	Down
30	Bronchitis	Depression
20	Pneumonia	Breakdown
10		
00	Death	Suicide

Intellectual, emotional and spiritual ageing brings opportunities for maturity for most people. Physically there is some decline. In fact physically we peak in our early twenties. This is particularly noticeable in some sports, like gymnastics. From the twenties on, the decline is so gradual as to go largely unnoticed. In fact performance may even appear to increase but this is due to people not realising their full potential in earlier years. In the fifties certain signs can begin to appear, such as odd twinges of stiffness, slight aches and pains, greying of hair and certain sexual changes. These changes are normal and need not impinge hugely on our awareness or activity. However from 75 onwards more noticeable alterations occur. Many of the body's systems and organs work less efficiently, for example eyes, ears, heart, lungs, kidneys, joints and muscles. Yet even then, with care and good management of limitations, an appropriate level of physical wellbeing can be achieved.

This chapter concentrates on areas of physical health over which we do have a say as to which behaviours we adopt. Special problems which arise due to disease or injury, which can occur at any age, but which are more likely to happen in the older years, are dealt with in chapter four on 'Living positively with disablements'. For most people in the second half of life, including those with chronic problems, the following points need to be borne in mind. Common sense, particularly in the areas of personal wellbeing, needs to be kept to the fore. To be avoided is an unhealthy preoccupation with physical health where people verge towards becoming hypochondriacs. There is today a cult of the body that can advocate exaggerated practices – fitness fanaticism, extremes in diets and exotic beauty-care techniques. Common sense is the best indicator of what is appropriate healthy behaviour to meet the needs of each individual

Three following key areas are explored in greater detail:

1. Rest, Exercise, Posture

2. Nutrition

3. Abuses

1. *Rest, Exercise, Posture*

a) Rest

All our bodily systems need rest, as does our psyche. Rest and sleep are different realities. As we age we need more rest and less sleep. Some people are fortunate in being able to retain their sleep pattern of the average norm which is around seven hours into their later years. Others will find their sleep time decreases. Unless it goes below four to five hours it is not normally something that requires medical attention. Sleep itself is a restorative process which most systems need, especially the brain which requires time for both resting and re-organisation. The electrical activity of the brain varies during sleep, showing that there is an active phase, where it is thought that the brain sorts itself out by shifting information around. There is also the rest phase. Both are necessary. The resting phase of sleep in an older person may not always reach the REM or deep sleep phase, so waking more often during the night (frequently due to bladder emptying) becomes more likely. This for many is part of the normal ageing process and need not cause alarm.

Rest as opposed to sleep, is an absence, or more accurately a minimisation of physical activity which allows the heart, lungs, and other organs, especially the muscles and joints, to relax following a period of exercise. Our exercise tolerance decreases with age and so fatigue levels can rise unless activities are planned to allow for more rest periods in between. Fatigue is a factor which requires some attention. Fatigue can interfere with a number of functions: it lessens physical efficiency during activity, dulls awareness, lowers concentration and can lead to accidents, especially falls. Getting up late in the morning is not the ideal, unless your pattern is to go to bed very late. A rest after lunch is recommended, preferably on top of the bed or on a suitable couch. It is good simply to relax and not necessarily sleep at this time, for fear of interfering with night sleep.

Positions of rest require consideration and choice of beds and chairs is important. A good bed needs a firm mattress and to be the correct height for its occupant. There is not an ideal chair for everyone, and, as with a bed, it needs to be suited to individual requirements. Unless stiff hips are a problem, you should be able to sit well back in a chair, with both feet on the ground while maintaining a right angle at hips, knees and ankles; hence the height of the chair is important. The seat of the chair needs to be comfortable but firm and be neither too deep nor too narrow. Ideally, we should not sit for longer that one hour at a time.

b) Exercise

The human body is made for movement. Primitive man spent the day largely active, hunting for food. Present western society has become far more sedentary. Many children are brought to school by car, people use transport to work, buildings have lifts and thus divert from the excellent activity of stair climbing. The supreme example of our sedentary, yet so-called efficient, culture is time spent in front of screens – iPad, iPhone or TV - with multiple forms of remote control buttons or switches. Some people try to counteract a sedentary lifestyle with weekend activities such as sport and gardening. A better way to ensure a sense of physical wellbeing is to take a reasonable amount of exercise each day.

As we age the same principle of daily exercise is necessary – only even more care is needed. An appropriate level of agility, strength and stamina should be aimed for but not strained at. Little and often becomes more the norm as we age. There are endless forms of exercise – the activities of daily living, walking, specific exercises, different types of sport or other leisure activities. All forms are encouraged if suited to your age and health status. Joints become stiff, muscles weak and the circulation sluggish from inadequate daily activity.

Fitness is an essential aspect of physical wellbeing. Children, those in their eighties, people in wheelchairs, or those with other limitations, should all aim at a reasonable level of fitness. Fitness has three components. The first of these is flexibility, which means maintaining as full a range of movement as is possible for all joints in the body. Ideally, we should try to put all joints through their full range a few times a week. This is a simple thing to do and need take no longer than five minutes. The second element is strength, which means keeping our muscle tone in good order and this can only be done through exercise. The third factor is stamina. This involves knowing how to pace oneself during activity, as well as over the sum of the day's activities. If we are unfit, we need to increase our exercise tolerance gradually. The older the person is, the more gradual the rate of increase must be. When an individual arrives as a level where they feel comfortably fit, the task then is to maintain that level.

c) Posture

Posture is both a static and dynamic reality. Our body is always in some particular posture, whether we are in bed, sitting or involved in some activity. In the older years, and particularly with women who are more prone to osteoporosis (softening of bones), the spine can become stooped. Awareness of this fact, with medication if required, plus making the effort to maintain adequate positioning of our body in sitting, lying and in activity, is desirable. Extra care needs to be taken when lifting or carrying objects. We should never attempt to lift more than we are safely able to cope with. Even one mistake could prove disastrous. Particular activities may become possible: for example, by halving loads and making two journeys, or carrying out tasks in stages.

2. *Nutrition*

Everyone needs a balanced diet. We also need to maintain weight levels that are suited to our size and body structure. Overweight is a real problem for several reasons. It prevents adequate fitness levels being achieved, puts a strain on the heart and weight-bearing joints, and makes a person at higher risk if surgery is required. Most people do not feel good in themselves when overweight. Research indicates that if we want to live longer we need to eat less as we age. This is common sense since as activity levels drop, less energy is required. If the food energy, commonly known as calories, is not used up by activity, the surplus is stored as fat in the body.

People can also be too thin for what is normal for them and this also diminishes a sense of wellbeing. It means usually that resistance levels are lower, and there is greater susceptibility to infections and disease, as well as insufficiency of energy even for normal activities. Putting on or losing weight means that clothes no longer fit well, and this is likely to make us feel less good about ourselves. Clothes are, so to speak, an extension of ourselves and as such they can add or subtract from a sense of wellbeing.

The fluid intake of older people, especially those in the 80+ years, needs to be watched. There can be a tendency to drink less, particularly if there is a problem of incontinence. Restricting fluid is not the way to manage this problem. Approximately eight average cups of liquid a day is considered the norm. Alcohol requires to be taken in moderation as the liver has greater difficulty in metabolising chemical substances. Moderation is needed in all forms of drug taking. For the older person medical drugs may be prescribed in lower dosages.

3. *Abuses*

Abuses in all areas of behaviour are, as in other age groups, unhelpful, sometimes harmful and most certainly cut across a sense of wellbeing. There are different categories of abuse for example:

- taking too much of any food or drink or indulging in harmful addictive substances such as nicotine, alcohol or other drugs;
- not taking drugs as prescribed;
- taking unnecessary risks in activities such as driving, gardening, sport or other hobbies;
- using poor lifting techniques;
- constantly adopting poor postures;
- being careless about fatigue levels which can result in one becoming accident-prone;
- being lax in regard to the safety in your environment, like ignoring worn, wet, or uneven floor surfaces;

- leaving trip hazards around, inappropriate arrangement of furniture, poor lighting, inadequate heating;
- goods in everyday use placed on high shelves;
- bathrooms without the necessary aids such as rails and non-slip mats.

A rough estimate says that one third of admissions of older people to hospital are due to falls, one third to taking or not taking correct medications, and one third to other factors such as illnesses.

⊛ END OF LIFE ISSUES THAT REQUIRE CONSIDERATION

As we move further into our older years it might be beneficial to think about three issues – Power of Attorney, Resuscitation and Living Wills. If one was to suffer from dementia it is good to have *Enduring Power of Attorney* previously established and this has to be done through a solicitor. This requires setting up a legal document where you decide whom you want to look after your affairs if you are unable to do so yourself. *Resuscitation* is a more difficult matter. At present when people are under the care of medical personnel, they are obliged as a general norm to resuscitate persons whose heart has stopped beating. If you do not want this to happen all one can do is to have a note in your hospital chart saying so and this statement has to be signed by yourself and a doctor. *Living Wills* are under discussion at present in Ireland. Legislation termed 'Advanced Healthcare Directives' (AHDs) is in place but not yet implemented. In the interim forms can be procured from the Irish Hospice Foundation where one can state one's personal wishes regarding end of life care. These wishes need to be in writing and include your own as well as a witness signature.

Intellectual wellbeing

There is a need to be more consciously aware of intellectual wellbeing as ageing progresses. A big problem for some people as they age is a narrowing of interest, which can result in one's world becoming very small. This is both unhealthy and sad when, with some foresight, it could have been prevented.

Except in a minority of persons, who are suffering from dementia, the intellect remains intact. Memory may drop somewhat particularly regarding names of people and places. An inability to recall recent events in detail may also be noticed in an older person. However the more important powers of the intellect, such as the ability to make judgements, to be reflective, to have an opinion, to learn new knowledge, to be creative, remain alive. Reaction time may minimally slow down but most people remain alert, especially if that extra moment is allowed for and particularly when taking in new information or trying to work out a problem. Maintaining, and more positively developing, a sense of intellectual alertness can be achieved in many ways and some suggestions are explored here under three headings: stimulating activities, setting goals, enlarging vision.

a) Stimulating activities

As with our physical self, it is important to 'stretch' our intellect, to include 'mental jerks' in our daily routine. There are endless ways of stimulating mental alertness: reading, study, entertainment, conversation, crosswords, bridge, chess and quiz programmes. In recent years more older people are going to universities. Degree courses of all kinds, some using the facilities of online methods of study, are possibilities open to mature students.

Some people, especially those with a largely functional mentality, query the purpose of continuing education for older people. While one aspect may be to skill or re-skill older people so that they can contribute further, either in the labour force or in voluntary groups, the main focus is more likely to be that of personal development/ enrichment. The recent development of the Men's Shed movement has helped many to restore, or learn afresh, a variety of skills. Often projects undertaken demand a team approach and this in turn benefits socialisation.

Watching endless TV is undesirable. A survey in England showed that the average number of viewing hours per week for those of 65 was 39 hours. It is unlikely that all this time was stimulating. In fact, too much unselected TV watching can have a deadening effect. Such a practice is a habit that can develop out of boredom and a lack of creativity in developing new interests. Interests that have an intellectual component are particularly helpful for intellectual wellbeing. Having the courage to try out new things is desirable, as well as having the persistence to try again if these fail. It is important not to narrow our interests too much in one area no matter how absorbing that might be. For example, if our sole interest is reading, or watching sporting programmes on TV and eyesight fails, the result can be devastating. The same applies to listening to music, if we become deaf.

A particular sport or craft may become the sole focus in our life, but if mobility is reduced or hand dexterity is diminished so as to interfere with such activities, we can become very despondent without alternative interests. It is clearly necessary to pursue a reasonably broad range of interests as a preventative measure, variety in itself being an asset that enlarges our capacity to enjoy life in greater fullness. By broadening our interests, conversation with others will be more interesting and as a consequence we will be more companionable and interesting to talk to and to be with. Keeping in touch with key world affairs can have a broadening effect and can be an antidote to our personal inner world becoming small or impoverished.

Being creative, possibly unleashing this side of ourselves for the first time, can be a great source of enrichment and joy. Doing things for others is an excellent form of stimulation.

b) Setting Goals

Passivity is one of the enemies of intellectual wellbeing. Keeping our power of choice, ability to make decisions, holding with confidence our opinions, as well as taking control of our life are all abilities to be held onto as we age. Intellectual energy, which includes thought-out strategies for ourselves, averts the likelihood of moving into a drifting-along type of existence. Effort is required to set goals for the future, be it for the day, the week, the month or even years ahead. Some people find this comes naturally; others may have to work more consciously at it. In summary, having a sense of purpose in life is crucial and contributes directly to the level of wellbeing we experience.

c) Enlarging vision

One of the gifts of the older years is having the time to realise, maybe only partially, some of the dreams of earlier years. We can also indulge the opportunity to dream afresh or rediscover dreams that have laid dormant deep within ourselves. Letting ourselves dream then gradually giving meaning to that dream by grounding some aspect of it into reality can be personally enriching. It can also surprise us. Important aspects of ourselves lie in our deepest desires, and unearthing this part of us can be liberating. This links well with the words of the poet Robert Frost: "For I have promises to keep and miles to go before I sleep."

Keeping in touch with new thinking is helped by keeping in tune with current affairs. Contact with children and youth can also be enlivening and keep us open to the 'new'. A closed mentality limits intellectual wellbeing and can often result in discontent and unhappiness. Constantly trying to enlarge vision allows for a broadening of our thinking and this in turn inevitably becomes a 'freeing' experience. The pathway that brings us closer to the truth, which is intellectual fulfilment, comes through a combination of stimulation, dreaming and reflection. This journey or process is endless since there is always more to discover.

Emotional Wellbeing

Emotional wellbeing is a complex reality and is difficult to write about since its boundaries are so indefinable. Emotional needs vary greatly throughout life for each individual and often they are the least well met of all our needs. Insufficient attention has been given to understanding emotional health, even by professionals whose caring work is concerned with the general good of their client or patient. This lack of attention is true for all age groups but it is particularly noticeable among older people who can often be left to their own devices. This could be so because either older people are expected to know how to cope in this area, or because emotional wellbeing is not considered as important as we get older. Nothing could be further from the truth. Indeed this is a period of life where emotional wellbeing needs to be thought through with extra care since so many negative factors can arise. Emotional difficulties vary but key ones are: a reduced sense of self-worth, insecurity, loneliness, sexual diminishment, and losses of varying kinds.

Certain realities that make for wellbeing will be looked at under the following headings:

- keeping alive and developing further our sense of self-worth
- maintaining a sense of belonging
- learning the art of giving and receiving
- learning the art of saying 'goodbye'
- working through negative feelings
- sexuality

a) Keeping alive and developing further our sense of self-worth

Wellbeing is a subjective reality; it is about how we experience life and how we view ourselves. It is concerned with feelings, with what affects us personally. To a large extent our personal experiences flow from the image we have of ourselves. If this tends towards the negative in a consistent way then self-esteem will be low. If this is the case, it is vital that we work at enhancing our sense of self-possession since this is the foundation for feeling good in our deeper self. It is nice and most helpful if others boost our self-worth by affirming it. This however is a bonus factor. The basic affirming of ourselves must come from oneself. Affirming, believing in ourselves as a person of value, is an essential prerequisite to living life to the full. This is so because while we can dislike things outside of ourselves, if we reject ourselves we reject that which keeps us alive.

In order to change from a position of self-rejection we need to stop making negative judgements about ourselves. It is the thoughts we have about ourselves that determine our self-esteem and especially the continual listening to negative thoughts that does the damage. Changing our thought patterns alters the way we feel and consequently behave. This is not easy, but it is possible to achieve. Those who have difficulty might benefit from counselling or participating in personal development courses. There is great potential for growth in all periods of life and many in recent years, especially women's groups, have found that this can be fostered through groups whose aim is to develop growth in self-knowledge while at the same time challenging people to look at new possibilities for living. Similar type groups could prove very helpful for older persons.

Our self-image is undoubtedly affected by the attitudes of others, be they from society in general or the significant others in our life. In particular, we can be powerfully influenced by professionals whose services we may seek. All of these categories of persons can enhance or diminish our self-image, although the most powerful force of all is the view we have of ourselves. If this is strong, a person can withstand a great deal of opposition and/or rejection and not be diminished by it. There is also the need not to allow oneself be unduly affected by the many forms of outside influences. The media and advertising industry can portray older people in a negative way and this can colour our perceptions. Magazines, for instance, are largely geared towards the young or middle aged and could lead to us saying almost imperceptibly to ourselves, 'we older people are not important. Society is not interested in us anymore, they see us as useless'. Even certain literary classics such as the works of Chaucer, Shakespeare, Swift and others often wrote pejoratively about the older years.

Self-esteem can further be coloured by the attitudes we have towards our own ageing. These attitudes will inevitably be connected to the thought patterns we have adopted over time. If these are negative, this fact alone will profoundly affect our feeling of self-worth. Self-esteem can also drop if it has been linked too closely with our role in life. If this happens and that role is relinquished, for example as teacher, manager, plumber, priest, politician, homemaker or whatever, then self-worth can plummet. True self-affirmation is based on valuing ourselves for who we are and not for what we do. Valuing our story is part of the self-affirming process. This means accepting the failures of the past and more importantly taking pride in our achievements. In a sense we *are* our story, and consciously 'owning' it at times can be helpful. Connecting with our personal history, with its ups and downs, joys and sorrows is all part of living with fuller awareness. Our goals and desires for the future also flow from all the life experiences that made that story.

b) Maintaining a sense of belonging

Self-worth alone is not sufficient to maintain wellbeing. We are social by nature and so maintaining bonds with people is necessary throughout life. Loneliness can be a problem for some older people. Ideally prevention is the best approach, but if a sense of isolation is present something needs to be done. Our world of relationships can tend to get smaller since losing family and friends through death is more likely. Connections we had with people at work or in other activities also tend to wane. This need not remain this way. The social dimension of life can actually improve through clubs, associations of all kinds and the creation of new friendships.

Whatever situation we find ourselves in, it is important to keep significant relationships alive. Maintaining contact with people, through the phone, writing, visiting, being open to receive visitors, using Skype/Facetime or email are to be encouraged, even if at times this requires effort. Effort may also be needed to maintain healthy dialogue with those we are close to or live with. As in other periods of life, relationships can become stale, or alternatively can flourish into having a new lease of life. Relationships, especially valued ones, need to be worked at all through life.

A sense of belonging can flourish if there is a strong sense of connectedness to a group and this could include larger groups such as nation, church and the world community. Even a hermit needs to have a sense of belonging. Indeed, a more profound one is necessary to sustain him or her in the solitary life.

Linked with the sense of belonging is the need of celebration. The celebratory side of life is important at all stages of life, and it is difficult if not impossible, to celebrate on our own. Various events in life call for celebration. A lack of 'play', lightheartedness, rejoicing with others, tends to make life dull and monotonous. We need the relief, the excuse at times, to break from our normal routine. A capacity for enjoyment plays an important part in a fulfilled life and celebrations are a delight-filled way to keep this side of life alive. Those blessed with a keen sense of humour are particularly fortunate.

c) Learning the art of giving and receiving

Both of these 'art' forms require thought, practice and fresh approaches as we age.

⊛ RECEIVING

It is true that most people find it easier to give then receive. Some people, and especially those who have a great need to be needed by others, find it particularly difficult to receive, whether it is a compliment, gift, gesture or service. The ability to receive graciously is an art, which has the value of benefiting both giver and receiver. The true receiver is one who accepts what is offered (assuming it is appropriate to do so) in a spirit of gratitude, being grateful for both the act itself and the concern shown behind it. Acceptance also involves humility. The proud person can receive but they are liable to see the gift as something that enhances their status. The humble person accepts in a way that enhances the giver. Humility and simplicity in the receiver is more likely to make the giver feel good and this can have the effect of enlarging the giver's spirit of generosity even further.

As we age it is likely that there will be some tasks that

we may need help to accomplish. The more intimate the task, the more difficult it can be to receive help. However, if the art has been practised in easier things, then when the more difficult situations arise there will be a greater facility to accept the necessary help.

❀ GIVING

An essential element in achieving fulfilment in life is to retain the ability to give to others. Due to possible limitations that the older years may bring, be it of purse, physical mobility or other reasons, more creative ways of giving need to be developed. The basic giving is the giving of respect to the person or people we are with; being aware of their needs as well as our own. As energy levels fall, there will be the temptation to excuse ourselves, and shirk the responsibility to go on giving. If this does occur, we ourselves suffer. Our world will become smaller and more self-centred and this in turn makes us more difficult to be with. In the older years the form of giving is likely to change, shifting more into the area of thoughtfulness and gratitude and less to that of activity. There are still endless ways to give; being as present as possible to others when they are with us; listening with attentiveness; remembering things of importance in the life of others; showing a concerned interest in their world; lovingly challenging a person when that seems the compassionate thing to do; giving a smile; thanksgiving – all are genuine and valuable forms of giving that are open to everyone.

d) Learning to say 'goodbye'

One of the keys to full living is developing an ability to cope with loss. Loss comes to us in many ways and includes people, pets, places, activities, personal functional abilities and dreams. When reality shows us that certain things are no long possible for us, it is desirable to move towards acceptance of this fact and not live in the unreal world of false hopes. Saying goodbye means letting go of what is lost and moving on to living fully within the present situation as it really is.

The necessity of saying goodbye to people who have died is obvious and this is achieved through the process of grieving. Other losses, especially the major ones like broken relationships, deep disappointments, personal inability to carry out favourite or essential tasks, having to leave one's home, also call for grieving. Loss of anything major usually affects several areas of life and so time is required to adjust to the altered situation. This could mean months or possibly a year or more, depending on how severely the loss affects an individual. The secret of fulfilled living for everyone is to work towards acceptance of both major and minor losses. This can only be done through the painful process of grieving.

It is our reaction to incidents such as loss that causes us the upset we feel. Reaction to loss is likely to move through the recognised phases of denial of the loss to begin with, then bargaining can occur. This can be with oneself, others or God. This period is often followed by anger and despair, until finally a person moves to the beginning of acceptance. This process is not a neat one and people tend to move backwards and forwards through the various phases. When some level of acceptance is arrived at, then we are able to shift our energy from constantly fighting the pain of the loss to concentrating on what is possible in the new situation that follows the loss. At this point, fuller living begins again.

Saying goodbye is also about letting go of all the 'could-have-beens', and realising the positive dimensions of the present. Those who make this transition can discover that life becomes fulfilling again, maybe even more fulfilling. Since loss is concerned with parting, it is always painful. The only way forward to finding meaning and joy in life again is to work through the pain. Leaving a hobby we have enjoyed for years, letting go of long-held ideas about things or ways of doing things, giving up independence regarding certain activities, are all difficult realities which may need to be faced in our later years. It is precisely by meeting the challenge, letting go of what is treasured, and moving to the altered situation with hope and an exploring spirit that sets out to discover what is positive in the new, that quality living will begin again. Ideally, this process is best worked through with the support of other people.

e) Working through negative feelings

The challenge and necessity of working through negative feelings is life-long. In the older years the source of such feelings is likely to come in three ways. Firstly, there is the unfinished business of the past. Secondly, there are the fears and anxieties connected with the future. Thirdly, there are one's reactions to the unpleasant happenings of present reality.

As we age, incidents of the present, or personal reflection on life in general, may release negative feelings connected with our past life. Some of these may never have been faced, or maybe were swept under the carpet. Others could have been so deeply buried as not even to emerge into consciousness up to this. Past hurts, deep resentments, disappointments, bitterness and unresolved anger, may surface. Such feelings can be triggered in quite unexpected ways. It these feelings are not faced and attempts made to work through them, they can remain a dark cloud, an irritant, which will cut across our sense of wellbeing and possibly lead to depression. Excessive anxieties and fears regarding the future can also take an unhealthy hold on us. A sense of realism, an anchoring of our life in the present is the best way to cope with such feelings. The future is unreal, and the fears envisaged may never come about.

Talking over our anxieties and fears – as well as the negative feelings connected with the past – with a trusted person can be helpful. If such feelings persist, professional help may be necessary. This should not be considered a luxury. Admitting to such a reality and taking appropriate action shows strength. People seek attention for physical ailments. Emotional ailments can be just as much, if not more, crippling.

There also may be need for self-forgiveness. Difficult as it may be to forgive others, forgiving ourselves can be even harder. Looking back over our life, there are likely to be some regrets, either of deed or omission. We can regret certain things we said or did which we would prefer we had not said or done. We can regret also the things we could have done or said, but did not do or say. Holding onto such regrets or failures as we may now perceive them is undesirable. Learning from them, making amends if this is possible and considered appropriate, and moving into the 'now' of life is what is necessary for emotional good health.

f) Sexuality

Wellbeing is closely linked with our sexuality. A sense of aliveness flows from a person being comfortable and in tune with their femininity, masculinity or bisexual self.

Being aware of our sexual self is an important part of fulfilled living in the older years as it was in our middle year period. If the sexual side of ourselves is let atrophy, part of what lies deepest in us is no longer able to give us life. The spark, or more aptly the sparkle of living, is no longer alight and as a result living can become drab.

Sexuality is intimately connected with our sense of self-worth. All relationships are coloured by the feelings we have about our own attractiveness or lack of it. Society today in this regard has tended to favour older men, in the sense that they are often seen as distinguished when the grey hairs and wrinkles appear. Women, partially due to commercial pressures, often try to do all they can through colours and creams to hide such signs. There is nothing wrong with this, as long as the focus is not only on physical appearance. Real attractiveness comes from within – from an alive personality that values and expresses one's womanhood or manhood.

As we enter our older years, we may need to consider what sex means to us. Our sexual life, as with other aspects of living, changes over the years. The sex drive is less intense than in the earlier years. We cannot recapture the type of sexual satisfaction of youth or the middle years later in life, but that does not mean it is no longer important. Sexual satisfaction is now different. It can be extremely fulfilling if it is kept to the fore as an important part of personal living. While it can and does include sexual intercourse for partners into the seventies or even later, it does mean for many couples opening up, and maybe discovering for the first time, the deep pleasurable experiences that can be found in a broad range of activities. There are many ways of making love, or giving and receiving sensual pleasure that result in deep emotional satisfaction.

'Pleasuring' is a term sometimes used regarding sexual fulfilment and by this is meant any sexual experience that makes us feel good. Small gestures of tenderness such as stroking, hugging, kissing, even a look or a smile, can all convey sexual meaning for people. Genital intercourse can be extremely satisfying if time is allowed for relaxation and intimate foreplay and if both persons are sensitive to the particular needs of the other. Many are ignorant about what to expect regarding their own sexuality and that of their partner. Sexual interest, performance, needs, alter and for sexual life to continue to be fulfilling it is necessary to be aware of the changes in both oneself and one's partner. Sharing openly with each other about such changes helps greatly in coming to a mutual understanding of what modifications in practice and behaviour are needed. It would appear from recent research that some couples deprive themselves of practically all forms of sexual expression due to an inability to work through this period of sexual adjustment.

Some men in particular appear to find the transition difficult when their level of performance alters in their later middle years. They can fail to realise that such changes do not abolish their sexual powers. Fears of becoming 'impotent' at this stage are more likely to result from psychological impotency than physiological incapacity. An erection takes longer to develop and will not be experienced with the same level of intensity, but it can last longer than with a younger man. Ejaculation may or may not occur. Women, especially if they stay healthy, can remain sexually active for the whole of life. In fact, many women become more sexually active and less inhibited after the menopause. Sexual interest of older women can remain very much alive since they alter physiologically less than men. The most notable change is a reduction in vaginal lubrication (which can be helped by the use of a cream or jelly).

The major shift that is necessary to achieve sexual satisfaction in the older years is one of orientation – the realisation that it is the giving and receiving of mutual affection and pleasure that is the important reality. How this is achieved is secondary. The affirmation that comes from being intimately loved by someone, and being able to reciprocate with our own love of the other brings healing, growth, comfort and pleasure. The enjoyment and sustaining aspect of a deep sexual life in the older years is one of its great enrichments. Some say they have discovered that their sex life has become 'even better' in later life.

Sexuality is important also for those who are single, including those who now find themselves widows or widowers. Many widowers marry again, widows less frequently. The option of settling down in a new partnership is a possibility to be kept open for all who find themselves single. There are those who have opted to remain single for life, such as religious and others. But for all, no matter what our life circumstances or choices, keeping alive a sense of our sexuality is an important part of ageing 'well'. Remaining life-giving to others whether in the context of partnerships or friendships calls for an alive sexuality. Denying this side of ourselves, or letting it peter out so to speak, harms health and prevents full living.

Spiritual Wellbeing

It may seem strange to some that this section on spiritual wellbeing follows immediately on that of sexuality. But in fact these two realities are closely related. Both are linked with what is deepest and most intimate in ourselves. Spiritual wellbeing is rarely adverted to or thought about. Even the phrase itself could sound unfamiliar. Spirituality is concerned with realities such as truth, beauty and freedom. It also includes a religious dimension. Spiritual values tend to hold a more prominent place in our lives as we age, and one of the ways of enhancing spiritual wellbeing is the degree of openness of mind and heart that we bring to our older years. Some people appear to shrivel as they age; whereas others let their spirit self to become ever more expansive as the years go by.

The search for truth, for meaning, is present in everyone. It is about looking for answers while, at the same time, being able to live with the questions which tend, as life goes on, to multiply and outweigh the answers. Discoveries emerge from the continued search if carried out with honesty and a sense of realism. Such discoveries can lead to a more satisfying explanation of life's great questions as we try to probe, even enter these great mysteries. At the same time, trying to find answers to specific issues may prove ever more difficult. In a strange way life becomes more complex and yet more simple, and holding together these two opposites is one of the fruits of the wisdom of the older years. The more truth is discovered, the more it is searched for, since the very discovery has a power which leaves us unable to stop searching for deeper truth. Finding truth as a compelling quality draws us ever further into what it is that has been found. Truth changes our lives more than anything else. There are layers of meaning to human existence and exploring the truth of the real, especially as it touches us personally, is the way to gain insight into what it is to be truly human. I referred already to Florida Maxwell, who wrote about ageing when in her eighties. She says: "A long life makes me feel nearer the truth, it is a time of discovery. 'Of what?' I am asked. We must each find out for ourselves, otherwise it won't be a discovery."

A reflective person, with an enquiring spirituality, can pursue a growing desire to explore truth about the deeper meaning of life, with an openness which is enlivening. Such a spirituality can break through prejudices, narrowness and assumptions that were held sacrosanct for years. This can lead to an exhilarating sense of inner liberation. The truth sets us free. True spirituality is the way to enlarge the life of the human spirit, which if not challenged can atrophy into a life of apathy and diminishment.

The capacity to create and enjoy beauty can become keener and more delight-filled in our older years. The ability to appreciate beauty in fresh and new ways, unknown until now, is one of the great possibilities and is open to all. The enjoyment and awareness of beauty will be further developed in the chapter on 'The satisfactions of the older years'.

Breaking into greater degrees of inner freedom is one of the greatest gifts ageing can bring. Freedom is about perspective, where we no longer cling to, or are tied down by inessentials. It follows from answering the call to conversion, in this instance the conversion of perspectives. The conversion process leaves the human heart and mind free to soar, no longer being bound by previous restrictions that we are now able to let go.

Religious faith can become very important to people as they age, even if this side of life was on the fringe or even discarded for many years. A growing religious sense, more accurately termed the religious dimension of human experience, can come about through the growing realisation of our own mortality, and this can have a calming as well as a challenging effect. Just as deep suffering can open us to a power greater than ourselves, so too a deeper consciousness of the reality of our own death can have a similar effect. The 'power greater than oneself' will for many be termed God. Specific religions will articulate faith in God with certain differences, but the life of the mystics, those who live most deeply of all, shows us that a simplicity emerges which can soften the edges of differences between the great world religions. Etty Hillesum, when facing death in a concentration camp, wrote in her diaries: "Sometimes I try my hand at turning out small profundities, but I always end up with just one single word: God. And that says everything, there is no need for anything more ... life has become one long stroll with God."

Wisdom – intellectual, emotional, but especially spiritual wisdom emerges in those who are open to nourishing their spiritual wellbeing. Spirituality is a profound part of what lies deepest in us and more will be said about it in the final chapter.

CHAPTER 4

Living Positively with Disablement

Disablement is used here as an umbrella word to include diseases, disabilities, or disorders. All of these cause some form of interference in one or more of the following areas: normal body functioning, mental ability, behaviour. While the older years must not be equated with disablement, the reality is that some older people will be so affected. Trying to categorise disablements is difficult because the range of problems is so broad. *Diseases* can be acute or chronic, congenital or terminal. *Disability,* normally the result of some chronic condition, can encompass a variety of problems such as restriction of movement, impaired vision or hearing, altered function of a body system, or mental deterioration. *Disorder,* a term usually used in reference to behaviour, is a consequence of things like alcohol, or drug abuse, or mental disturbances such as anxieties or phobias.

An older person is liable to all forms of illness just like people of other age groups. Particular diseases become more prevalent – coronary heart disease, stroke, Parkinson's, arthritis, cancer, blood pressure problems, cataract, Alzheimer's and other forms of dementia. Anyone with a previous chronic problem such as a respiratory condition, arthritis, or schizophrenia, will inevitable have to contend with that as well as other problems that may arise. As we move into the 75+ age group, there is greater likelihood of having more than one condition to cope with as well as becoming more accident prone and generally experiencing an increasing level of frailty as we move into the mid-eighties.

The main focus in this chapter is on reactions, attitudes and management of disease, disability or disorder and not on strictly medical treatments.

Reactions

1. *Illness is a crisis-provoking event*

ESRI research has shown that people's main problem in the older years was not loneliness or lack of finance but the fear of illness and dependency. Undoubtedly the transition from full health to ill health - be it acute, chronic or terminal - is a crisis-provoking event. For people of all ages, the diagnosis of an illness constitutes a crisis unless the illness is minor and of a transient nature. Hearing of a major diagnosis pronounced on ourselves is an event that can have an even greater significance than some of life's other major crisis such as a loss of a spouse, retirement, relationship difficulties or children leaving home. The severity of the illness, one would assume, is the measure of the level of crisis. In fact, it is largely our subjective reaction, rather than the objective nature of the illness, that determines the degree of upset. The personal loss of morale that can occur predisposes a person to adopting an inappropriate and unhealthy lifestyle. Such a lifestyle change is often a drifting into apathy and lacks the element of challenge. Over time this adds further to low morale. Health personnel and services need to give more attention to the morale effect of illness, to facilitating its improvement, seeing this as an important part of their contribution to the recovery process. On the whole, there has been a lack of emphasis on developing coping mechanisms to help patients manage their condition constructively. The professional focus has solely been on trying to cure, to the detriment of time spent trying to enable patients to manage their own problems, guided by the knowledge and expertise which the professional freely shares. The overall 'treatment package' should include the giving of information about the nature and prognosis of the illness, as well as supplying ongoing education on the physical and psychological management of this unique person, with their specific problem, in their particular life situation.

2. *Receiving a diagnosis*

Receiving a diagnosis is a jolt to our body and mind – to our whole person. It can cut across a particular functional ability which most of us would have previously taken for granted. But it affects more than mere function; the whole of life – dreams, plans, relationships, the ability to do what we want to do could be affected in some way. An illness is sometimes experienced as a sentence, because at the heart of the experience are the acute feelings aroused by the thoughts of freedom being curtailed.

The moment of diagnosis provokes shock. If the disease manifests in an acute and serious form, it will give rise to profound uncertainty and confusion. Those who have been waiting months or longer to discover what is wrong may have suffered a great deal of anticipatory anxiety which can also lead to doubt and confusion. When the diagnosis is finally pronounced, such a person's immediate reaction may be one of relief: 'now at last I know what is wrong'. In such cases, the shock reaction is likely to be delayed until the reality of what is now finalised sinks in. When the shock stage subsides, negative feelings are likely to emerge as the implications of what has happened begin to dawn. Intense anger and/ or sadness are common feelings. Bargaining can take place – with self, others, God. What is happening is that the person is going through the process of grieving for the loss or losses that are most keenly felt as a result of the illness. This is natural and in a sense healthy. Over time, however, it is desirable that the person comes to complete the grieving process and arrives at some level of acceptance of what has happened. Some, alas, remain unaccepting of their situation, while others move to partial, or, best of all, full acceptance. Acceptance, partial or full, allows us to live again within whatever limitation has taken place. The amount of support and insightful help that is available over this period will play a major role in facilitating the person to come to terms with what has taken place.

3. *The acceptance journey*

On the journey towards acceptance, it may at first be difficult to see any positives in life. This is acceptable in the early stages of grieving, but it is imperative to turn away from this negative position, which also serves to hinder the recovery that is possible. Non-acceptance of what has happened usually includes an inability to face the prognosis in a realistic manner because pessimism clouds vision. Continuing to fight emotionally against the diagnosis and prognosis absorbs energy and makes full living impossible. From such people it is not uncommon to hear two particular phrases: 'If only...' or 'when I am better...', both revealing an outlook that is not rooted in reality. The 'if only' remark indicates distorted aspirations that are not earthed or connected to their present situation. This wishful thinking prevents a person looking at and experiencing the positive aspects, and there are always some present no matter how black things seem. 'When I am better' connects with the future which is always something unreal. Such a comment masks the truth. Often we know the truth deep down when we allow ourselves to be honest with ourselves. Gradually, there is need to face gently the challenge of what getting better means. It is a relative concept. People close to such a person can be unhelpful if they collude in the game of pretending that the person will recover according to their false desires, when they know better. Not telling the full truth is allowable and sometimes desirable, but pretence is unhelpful and hinders positive living. We are not obliged to speak 'the whole truth' in most circumstances in life, but this is very different from denying truth, from not facing what is real in a given situation. If the 'if only', or 'when I am better' syndrome persists, professional help, in the form of counselling may be needed. Facing truth does not destroy hope, as some people think. Genuine hope springs from being rooted in the truth of the present. It does not operate from pretence of falsehood.

4. *Different situations/Varied reactions*

Reaction to an illness is rarely a once-off thing. There are ongoing reactions as the path of the disease alters.

Different diseases take different courses. Some are progressive, causing symptoms which generally manifest as deterioration, the rate and degree depending on the condition in a particular person. Some are more constant, in that after the initial episode and the adjustment period, there then follows a time of stability. Other conditions are characterised by periods of a relapse or remission, with often unpredictable times of feeling well and relatively symptom-free, followed by the opposite.

Some diseases have a life-threatening dimension. However the good news is that, with advances in early detection and constant improvement in treatments, many of these conditions, including cancer, can be managed, even cured. Despite this fact, the reality is that most people diagnosed with a potential life-threatening illness live (as do the families) with some uncertainty. Such uncertainty is realistic, but a sense of realism also requires that fears be kept in perspective and in the background, especially as individuals get on with positively living their lives again as the months move to years and then to further years, even decades.

There are also some people whose reactions can be overly positive, in the sense that they become unrealistically optimistic about themselves in a way that is unhelpful, and maybe even harmful. Understanding is the way to finding a true and healthy balance which allows for realistic living that is neither overly optimistic or pessimistic.

While reaction to chronic illness has been the main focus discussed, the process is not dissimilar for those diagnosed with terminal disease. Due to the likely shortening-of-life element the shock will inevitably be greater. However the process of coming to terms with, and moving to living life as fully as possible in the now is even more important. With advances in palliative care in recent times and the holistic approach they offer at both out and inpatient levels, such situations are considerably eased for the both the ill person as well as their families. Apart from what has previously been said about approaches to serious diagnosis, in terminal care situations there may be the need to draw attention to the necessity of coping with any 'unfinished business'. Such business could be practical, emotional or spiritual. Completing this, at least partially, is often what enables a person to live fully the days, months or years that are left to live.

Acute illness forces us into the present. When someone is very ill, personal energy is largely spent on existing in the now of hopefully not too much pain, uncertainty and a general feeling of weakness and unwellness. Fears of the future, of death, may intrude, but the basic want is to be able to hold on until one gets through the acute stage of that illness.

Attitudes

1. *Taking responsibility for personal attitudes*

It would be nice for all of us if we could live without physical or psychological trauma all our lives. This of course happens to no one, yet there is a common assumption that it is not right when unpleasant things affect us personally. A reaction 'it's not fair', can in turn arouse the dangerous emotion of self-pity, which exclaims 'poor me' or 'why me?' While this reaction is understandable in the early days following a crisis, it is undesirable to remain in this mood. Our ability to move from it depends on how seriously we take responsibility for our own emotional states. If the 'poor me' attitude persists, it can result in the person knowingly or unknowingly taking refuge in the 'martyr' role. This approach is unhelpful and may even be destructive. It makes life miserable for ourselves and also those who are close to us.

2. *The search for meaning*

Ultimately our reaction to unpleasant happenings comes from our basic philosophy and spirituality. By spirituality I mean that part of us that gives personal meaning to ourselves, to all that happens to us whether it comes from within ourselves or from without. Grappling to find meaning is necessary, particularly during crisis times. It is desirable to try to discover meaning when a serious illness is diagnosed, that may cause us to believe that the beginning of a downward slide to greater ill health and dependency has commenced.

3. *Changing personal attitudes*

It is through a search for meaning and perspective that attitudes are born. They are formed over life, but we can change them if we are honest about facing truth and alter perspectives accordingly. Understanding, and insight, is the way to bring about change. Part of the understanding referred to here is the realisation that moments of crisis, while initially negative, contain also within them the possibility for personal growth. In other words, there is a positive dynamic inherent in everything, even in those realities that cause us physical or psychological pain. We can 'go to pieces' in crisis, or we can grow enormously, even to unleashing a potential in ourselves that we were unlikely to discover otherwise. Thus the crisis of disablement provides the possibility for either challenge or growth, or for disaster and despair. The event itself is not what decides which of these it will be; rather it is our attitude to what has happened, the way we perceive it, which dictates the orientation we adopt. It is not an either/or situation; many people's attitudes fluctuate along a continuum between the two poles of negative and positive. The important thing is to be able to shift attitudes, at least into the positive half (see diagram). The more positive attitudes become, the more likely fuller living will be experienced and this can take place in the midst of severe illness, be it acute, chronic or terminal.

Attitudes to Illness

−	+
Disaster	Challenge
Despair	Growth

If we have been positive about our ageing process, and if we are comfortable with our body, the trauma of illness is likely to be accepted more easily and with a greater sense of perspective. It will not be seen as the 'end of the world', as the end of the A-Z of life but simply as the end of XYZ. Genuinely facing up to and grieving for the loss of XYZ, and then letting go of the loss, or abilities that are no longer available, allows us to move on to concentrate on and enjoy the A-W aspects of life that remain. Some so bemoan the section they have lost that they are no longer able to see, let alone enjoy, what they still have. A prerequisite for allowing this move in attitude to take place is to have previously kept alive, and preferably even enlarged, our range of interests so that while following an incident of illness certain interests have to be forgone, there are still alternatives in place.

Unless, as we age, we have created for ourselves interesting things to focus on, a particular disablement is more likely to take hold of us in a way that preoccupies us and becomes more crippling than need be.

4. *Disorders*

The focus in this chapter so far has been illness and disability. Disorders can also interfere with our sense of wellbeing. These largely arise as a consequence of particular behaviours that upset a sense of balance in daily living. With mellowing of time, it is possible to look afresh at some of these disorders. For instance addictions such as smoking, drinking, drugs and gambling could overly dominate one's older years. It is never too late to give these up or at least limit their use; increased use is to be avoided. Over-indulgence in regard to food, as well as in relation to particular activities can also distort a holistic lifestyle and in addition limit personal freedom. Similarly excessive forms of behaviour, be they connected with relationships or other matters, are likely to diminish rather than enhance our lives.

Two factors can act as potent motivators in remedying these disorders: an attitude-shift which desires quality living in the older years, and an awareness of the possibility of an illness being worsened by continuing with such behaviours. The attitude: 'well, the harm is done, there is no point in changing now' is not based on factual evidence, since it is beneficial to health and wellbeing to make the required changes.

Management

1. An overview of managing disablements

Healthy attitudes form the basis of managing disablement. Good or bad management in turn influences attitudes. Management is about how best to cope with a particular disablement. It also includes how we manage our total life situation in relation to an ailment. While diseases, disabilities or disorders have common manifestations which make each identifiable, there are enormous variations within a particular condition. No two people have exactly the same symptoms or problems following a stroke, arthritis or whatever. What differentiates one person from another with a similar complaint is both the specific presentation of the illness in this particular person and their reaction, attitudes and ability to manage the problems that arise.

2. The ongoing nature of managing disablements

Management is practical – it is the 'how to' which enables us to cope with living. It allows us to maximise the use of existing abilities and to develop new ones. It also helps to prevent deterioration where possible. If deterioration does occur, then learning to cope with this changed reality is all part of management. Management is never something static. There is a constant ebb and flow with many illnesses – the acute and chronic stages, the flare-ups and remissions. Added to this is the possibility of multiple pathologies occurring. For instance, someone has a stroke and after time has learnt to accept and manage this difficulty. Then suddenly a respiratory problem arises. The effort to work a second time through the arduous journey from shock to acceptance may at first seem too much. However, the only alternative route is one which brings diminishment and is a form of opting out of life. The acceptance road is never easy, but there is no shortcut. Allowing the necessary time to make this journey has to be done since there is no instant method. Illness is a blow which can shake confidence. Regaining confidence in ourselves and in our ability to do things requires patience. It is helped greatly by the encouragement and support of others.

Some particular situations which require skilful and sensitive management.

Obviously, with conditions which have an element of confusion, the many and often distressing problems will have to be managed by others – a partner, sibling, children, friend or outside agency. Increasing numbers of people with intellectual disability are now surviving into old age. Their needs requite specialised care. Parents who have looked after their children who have a disability may find it difficult to continue doing so when they enter their own older years and no longer have the strength or health to continue. Great sensitivity is needed in such situations.

Management is called for in two areas of personal living – the physical or more practical side, and the psychological dimension.

3. *Practical Management*

a) Health services

All disablements require access to adequate health services. The range of services required will depend on the nature of the illness. Some may also require the benefit of the social services. The focus in this section is deliberately on the self-help aspect of management. However, included in managing ourselves is knowing when and how to go about receiving outside help when it is appropriate to do so. The core of all health services is the GP. Being able to relate openly and with confidence to your own doctor is of paramount importance. Appreciating the knowledge and expertise of an expert, as well as valuing your own, establishes a healthy partnership which is for your own good. Self-knowledge and professional knowledge should be viewed as complementary and never as competing. The numerous other services, be they hospital, in or outpatient, or community services, should be called on and utilised when necessary. Key personnel in community services are Public Health Nurses, Carers and Home Helps. In addition there are the more specialised services of Physiotherapists, Occupational Therapists, Speech Therapists and Chiropodists. Not to be forgotten is the very real help of relatives, friends, and neighbours. Such help can be both practical and supportive. It is very difficult to carry or manage a disablement entirely on a 'go-it-alone' basis.

The more personally any of the above services are delivered, the more beneficial they are likely to be. Apart from the expertise of medical care, the other qualities needed by service providers are adequate time, good communication and rapport. When delivering appropriate care to their patients, health workers also need to be motivators and teachers. Managing a condition requires first of all knowledge about that condition and also acquiring the necessary skills, and that can only be achieved through practice. Management programmes should ideally be initiated by experts, but over time a person learns ways and means of perfecting their own management techniques. A creative approach, having the courage which allows for mistakes and yet being able to learn from them, is a desirable quality to possess when managing disablements.

b) Some examples of managing particular disablements

Everyone's situation is unique, but the following examples could indicate what is meant by managing a particular disablement. If deafness occurs (depending on its type) there is need for ear tests, likely to be followed by a hearing aid which will take several weeks to become adjusted to. Avoid giving up using it too early on, use loop systems when available in public spaces like churches and at public lectures. Deaf people also need to adjust to many hidden aspects of their disability, especially if not wearing the aid, like not having the assistance of noise when crossing a street, learning to be more sensitive to the body language of others when one can no longer rely on words to pick up subtleties in human relating; coping with the adverse reaction of others' who may not always be as sensitive and tolerant as one would like to the problems and frustrations involved in hearing loss.

Incontinence problems necessitate management of the amount and timing of fluid intake and the use of incontinent wear if deemed necessary. Mismanaging problems could include a person not taking enough fluids, or stopping socialising for fear of an accident occurring. Good planning, like knowing where toilets are and timing of fluid intake should counteract difficulties when outside one's home.

c) Altering Lifestyle

Altering lifestyle is always difficult, especially for those who are attached to long-standing routines and methods of doing things. The adjustment required might be very minor or it could be something that has major implications. Examples would be when it is no longer possible to drive a car, use the stairs, see the TV, or when it is necessary to move into a nursing home. When all options around staying at home become too difficult, and residential care is required, the facilities of the home suggested should be looked into. For example does it allow for autonomy, privacy and intimacy? Could some aspects of personal care continue to be given by a close relative or friend if this is desired, and does a creative, pleasing and homely atmosphere prevail? Knowing the general ethos and philosophy of care in a particular nursing home is essential before a final choice is made.

Two key rehabilitation principles must be borne in mind on the question of assistance. The first is not to receive help before it is necessary, for example, if we can still carry out a task independently or are able to live independently in our own home. It may take longer to carry out a task, and the assistance of a mechanical aid(s) may be required, but the important thing, namely independence, is safeguarded. If help is needed, and this may be minimal or a great deal, then receive it graciously, showing concern for the person who supplies it. Surveys show that of the 20% of older people who have dependency problems only 5% have high dependency. A further 5% have low dependency needs such as someone to help with the shopping and other smaller tasks within the home. Safety is the crucial issue and is largely the deciding factor as to what level of care is appropriate.

d) Concern for the carer

If there is need for a carer, be they family or from an outside agency, it is vital to be attentive to the carer's wellbeing as well as your own. Over-demanding behaviour can be destructive in this vital relationship for the cared-for person. It is necessary to achieve a healthy balance between both sides of the caring relationship. The carer needs to avoid undue pressure, even bullying tactics, and the person receiving the care requires sensitivity in avoiding over-demanding behaviour which could evoke an abusive reaction. In other words, a spirit of reasonableness must prevail where freedom and personal responsibility are valued both for you and for the other person in this special caring relationship. For example, if the carer is a member of the family and needs a break, it is not unreasonable that the person cared for avail of some form of respite facility. While this idea may not be relished, acceptance of such care for a short period is reasonable. More difficult is the decision to move to palliative or nursing home care, should dependency or other medical needs become too difficult to manage at home. Realism, courage and openness are called for as to what is the most appropriate form of care as a particular illness or disability progresses, in relation to the resources that are available in the home and in the community. Placing unduly heavy demands on the personal lives of others is unreasonable. Many factors need to be considered when making a decision as to what is the most desirable form of care in a particular set of circumstances. Moving to a nursing home does not have to be seen as a last resort, 'a sentence' or the end of the world. Some people positively opt for such a move, maintaining a spirit of maximum independence in such a situation, and even discover opportunities for fuller living that were no longer possible for them while living at home. A spell in a nursing home may be a necessary stage in the final transition from home to nursing home care.

e) Personal involvement and responsibility in decision-making

Decisions regarding the different types of care, and even the pros and cons of particular treatments, are more and more discussed between health professionals and their patients. Responsibility in having a say, co-operating in difficult and often complex matters regarding our care, is something to be thought about in advance and is not a matter to be evaded as particular situations arise.

Involvement in our own care, maintaining personal choice (even if the range of options is more restrictive than one would like) is desirable. Effective management is not about handing over total control to others. However, making decision in this matter is often painful and requires adequate knowledge about the issues involved, as well as a degree of reasonableness towards yourself and the other people who will be affected by that decision.

f) Care of general health

Managing a disablement must also include care of our health in general. The preventative dimensions of care on issues in relation to fitness, adequate rest, appropriate weight level, as outlined in chapter two, need to be borne in mind. Part of general self-care is awareness – noticing changes that occur and attending to them in an appropriate way early on. 'A stitch in time saves nine'. An example of one area to notice and care for is our feet. Changes in skin colour, temperature, as well as toenails and breaks in the skin, can be significant. Often these are signs that show the early signs of circulation problems or diabetes. Foot-care requires suitable footwear, good hygiene and probably the services of a chiropodist. Another example is care of our teeth. Diminished swallow, coupled with poor eating habits could be aggravated by some form of dental problem.

g) Maintenance of aids

A further aspect of management is the maintenance of aids. Examples would include seeing to the general upkeep and suitability of hearing aids, especially batteries; that glasses and dentures remain suitable and in good condition, ferrules on a stick or frame are in good condition; truss, collar, back and other support wear are replaced when worn; motorised wheelchairs and other more specialised equipment are serviced at regular intervals.

h) Safety

Safety issues are all part of good management. Included is the management of risk. It is undesirable to take unreasonable risks, but we can become over-cautious. If life is seen as an adventure then risk is always involved. Some people get nervous about themselves after an illness, so being firm yet kind with ourselves, and taking small positive steps to rebuilding confidence, is the way forward. If there have been falls, these can be so inhibiting that a person almost stops walking. The encouragement of others, planning manoeuvres with care and a prudent spirit of daring is, over time, what works best. Safety management also includes the elimination of risk hazards in the house and not carrying out tasks that are unsuitable to one's condition.

i) Managing pain

Learning to cope with pain is also a management issue. If pain is acute, medical attention is required. Chronic pain and discomfort largely call for self-management. The type and nature of pain has often a recognised pattern known to the person, as also is its cause – most likely a particular diagnosis. Having a positive attitude regarding our ability to manage this pain, rather than letting the pain take control, is fundamental. Preventing chronic pain that interferes with living, demands common sense and self-talk to get it into perspective, as well as at times putting distracting activities in place. Pain that is consciously focused on and overly analysed often gets worse. Relief of chronic pain by the use of medication may be needed, but overuse of paracetamol or other 'over-the-counter' pain relievers should be avoided and replaced where possible with good self-help techniques such as distraction therapy, for example indulging in something we enjoy. Repositioning oneself may help in muscular/skeletal pain. The latter might include lying or doing tasks that ease the pain, not staying in any one posture for too long, doing tasks differently or in stages, taking rest periods, practicing some form of relaxation. We are fortunate today to have medical specialists who deal with severe pain management. In addition palliative care medicine is equipped to manage the severe pain that can arise in the end stages of cancer care.

4. *Psychological Management*

Managing the practical issues connected with an illness is often the easiest part. Managing ourselves, our feelings and thoughts, as well as our significant relationships, is more complex. If there is an intimate relationship, the whole area of sexual behaviour that might need to be altered has to be worked through with sensitivity by both partners in the relationship.

A fundamental matter in this regard is how we view our condition. Most illnesses are chronic and so a person is not really sick most of the time. The type of behaviour that results depends on perception. Some operate from well behaviour, others from sickness-type behaviour, and it is this basic difference that colours how we relate to ourselves and to others. Maintaining personal autonomy, freedom and the right to privacy are values to be insisted on, especially if those close to us tend to be over-protective. Being sensitive to others is also important and includes avoiding unduly excusing ourselves because of our condition. During moments of frustration, which will be inevitable at times, we need to be wary that this is not unfairly directed against those who are close. Remaining alert to the needs of others, as well to our own, is a balance that requires working at.

Older people who live alone can often be more resourceful, simply because there is no one around to do things for them. On the reverse side, however, such people can become recluses in a way that is not normal or helpful for them. Bad habits can develop which let efforts at personal self-care, as well as normal social functioning, slip.

Managing the emotional and relationship issues connected with a disablement are the most difficult to deal with and hence they are receiving fuller consideration in the following chapter on managing stress.

CHAPTER FIVE

Managing the Stresses of the Older Years

Stress is part and parcel of life, including the older years. It is our ability to cope with it that makes the difference between fulfilled and unfulfilled living. Learning to cope with the inevitable stresses of life involves understanding more clearly what stress is, what its effects are, and what are effective methods to cope with it.

What is stress?

The word *stress* has an engineering background. Materials are checked out under different stresses to discover their strength and durability. If the pressure or strain is too great, there is a point at which the material will bend, crack or break. The same idea is used when talking about personal inner strength. If the pressure or strains of life are too great to cope with, we can, in phrases commonly used, 'crack up' or 'break down'. It is difficult to define personal stress, but a possible definition is 'when we are pushed beyond comfortable limits'. Stress can cut across our sense of wellbeing to the extent that we no long feel comfortable with ourselves. There is a good form of stress which is normally termed challenge. Artists, sports people, those working in projects they are interested in, often benefit by being stretched to give their best. The stress referred to here is the bad form, namely, distress.

Often we are not sufficiently aware of our level of stress until it is quite severe. Trying to manage it then becomes increasingly difficult. When we are aware of our personal stress, we can pick up the warning signs early on. If we admit to it and do something early to remedy the situation, then much suffering can be prevented. The consequences of stress are many and varied, the predominant one being that a lot of joy goes out of living, with positive feelings receding and negative ones taking over. A severe result of uncoped-with stress is 'break-down' or 'burn-out'. Those who find their final years at work particularly stressful might enter their retirement period in a state of burn-out, which might call for a period of rest and possibly professional help before fuller living can emerge and the positive aspects to ageing begin to be appreciated and lived.

Our 'stress threshold' varies over life, even over one day. To an extent it depends on the multiplicity of stresses that can come together at any one time. We may be coping well with a major crisis and then something small happens, the threshold is crossed, and we can no longer manage. In other words, we have gone beyond our tolerable limit. Stress is present from the teenage years on, and each period of life, while containing the stresses common to all periods, has also its own particular stresses to contend with. If the art of coping with stress has been developed over life, then we are fortunate in having this skill to rely on when coping with the particular stresses of the older years.

Understanding the three sources of stress can be helpful:

❊ The first source is the environment, that is anything outside of ourselves, including places, things, people, circumstances or events. The physical surroundings in which we live can be pleasing or act as a stressor. An untidy kitchen, diminished personal living space, a dark room, a dirty house, drab buildings, lack of colour, no plants in a house or no trees in a neighbourhood, messy bins nearby, can all be potential stressors. However, relating to other people remains the most common source of stress. Personal circumstances and events can also act as profound stressors.

❊ A second source of stress, already noted, is our own body. If we are not comfortable with our body as it ages, then we live with a constant source of irritation. If there is some disease or disability in addition, and this is not accepted, then our body becomes an even greater source of stress.

❊ The third source of stress, and the commonest cause of it, is our own thoughts. Personal thoughts label how we perceive and interpret life's happenings. Places, events and relationships have no emotional content. It is our thinking which evokes the type of feelings that are aroused. Stress is often the result of 'twisted thinking patterns', such as prejudices, tunnel vision, black and white thinking, and exaggeration.

Our thoughts flow from our beliefs, values and attitudes. Beliefs change slowly and imperceptibly; core beliefs tend to last a lifetime. Regarding values, people notice that over the years their values change, sometimes radically, sometimes in small ways, and some values remain constant. Looking back over a decade or more, we discover possibly that values we previously held as sacrosanct are no longer so. Changes are noticed only over a period of time; the change as it occurs is largely imperceptible. Attitudes, on the other hand, can be changed more easily as we consciously set to work, challenging ourselves on some of our personal attitudes. This involves checking out with ourselves why we have adopted certain attitudes to see if they are true, fair to the person or situation as it really is. By deliberately standing back and objectively looking at ourselves in relation to people, circumstances, or events, we can decide to alter particular attitudes. The change is not easy. It happens for us in the very act of understanding, as we stand back and see things in new and different ways.

Stresses arise from different types of situations:
In the first place are sudden unexpected events like

an accident, an illness, a death of someone close. It is appropriate at such times to be under stress, but it is also normal to work through this stress in a reasonable period of time.

Another category can be those associated with entering a fresh period in life such as a new job, retirement, leaving one's home, maybe to living with a relative or to a nursing home. Learning to live with a disability is in this second category, as well as learning to cope with the disability of a spouse or other close family relative with whom one lives. It takes time to adjust to the new situation. It requires us to be gentle with ourselves as we move into an altered lifestyle.

There are the minor stresses of everyday life, like difficulties in relationships, worrying about one's children or grandchildren, financial concerns etc.

Finally, the unconscious self can be a source of stress. Hidden anxieties, fears, hurts, can emerge at any stage throughout life and especially in our older years, when the unfinished business of our earlier years calls for attention. Such buried feelings can be resurrected unexpectedly by almost anything, such as at the death of a sibling, even by looking at old photographs. Some feelings may have been buried since childhood, when they were too difficult to face. Help may be necessary to cope with these and other feelings connected with the darker side of our past.

There is a close connection between our mental and physical health. For example, if we have the flu, or have broken a bone, we will feel down in ourselves at least at times during the period of recovery. The period of convalescence may prove more difficult than the acute phase. Conversely, if we are psychologically low, for example following bereavement, we are more prone to physical ailments. It is now generally accepted that the psychosomatic dimension can play a part in illness. Recovery from sickness or learning to live with a disability takes longer and is less complete if there are stresses not adequately coped with.

The first stage in coping with stress is to be aware that we are under stress and take responsibility for this fact. Following on from that it is helpful to be able to identify the source(s) as specifically as possible. For instance, to say one's stress comes from a relationship, or one's physical environment, or a particular disablement is too general. There is a need to find out what precisely are the factors in the situation that make it bothersome and to name these.

The effects of stress

The effects of stress are numerous and vary from person to person. Being aware of the early onset of stress, by knowing our personal signs and symptoms (triggers), can help minimise its effects, provided such signs are taken seriously and we do something to alleviate the situation. The more common signs and symptom can be categorised under physical, emotional and intellectual aspects of our lives (categories already familiar when speaking about wellbeing). Several symptoms are likely to appear if the stress is severe.

Physical symptoms include the following: tiredness which is not related to levels of activity; sleeplessness, either going to sleep with difficulty or wakening early; headaches (sometimes referred to as tension headaches); stomach pains; chest tightness; vague aches and pains, especially in the neck and shoulders; palpitations; breathlessness and sweating. Such symptoms could mean there is an underlying physical disorder which would require checking with the doctor. If, however, nothing is discovered and you are in a known stressful situation and this symptom has been noticed before in other stressful periods, then stress is likely to be the cause of these symptoms and treatment is required to manage the stress.

Emotional symptoms which are commonly experienced when under stress are: feeling edgy, irritable, drained; negative feelings predominating; inability to manage your feelings as you normally would, crying becoming intense sobbing; failing to overcome emotional upsets in a normal time span, where for example anxiety, anger, sadness linger or where our reaction is out of proportion to the cause, such as losing your temper over some small incident.

Intellectual symptoms can be significant and they include: inability to concentrate; listlessness; racing thoughts; preoccupation with the traumatic event; lack of interest in things; a general sense of apathy; nightmares.

Spiritual symptoms can also act as indicators of stress. These can include: a persistent inner restlessness; searching for meaning in events and in your own life; unconnected outer and inner self; life not in tune with your inner desires; wrestling with suffering and pain (physical and emotional); scruples.

Changes in normal patterns of behaviour could indicate the presence of stress. For instance, addictive behaviours usually increase – a person drinks, or smokes more than is normal. Eating habits can alter –some eat more, others less. Some people become tight with money, others overspend. It is not uncommon to find older people who are overly concerned about money and constantly check their financial affairs. This could be stress-related or an early sign of dementia. A lack of attention to personal appearance might indicate the presence of stress. If stress is severe a person can become withdrawn.

Knowing *the signs of stress in a relationship* can be helpful. Such signs could be showing an absence of gestures of affection that previously were normally shown; entering a pursuing/distancing cycle in the relationship; small problems becoming catastrophes; having difficulty in acknowledging needs without blaming the other person.

Why some physical symptoms appear as a result of stress is due to the way our bodies work. There are two systems involved in a stress situation: the nervous system and the endocrine or gland system. In acute stress, an alarm reaction is aroused in the body and this is sometimes called the fight/flight response. The body does not distinguish between stress and fear, so when under stress the body reacts as if it had a fright and hence the fight/flight reaction is aroused. Because of circumstances and conditioning we tend to do neither. However, the alarm warning has gone off and this results in a higher level of adrenalin in the body which has certain effects. It causes the heart to beat faster and blood pressure to rise. Breathing quickens and muscles tightened ready to spring into action. Without such action the tightness tends to settle in three areas: the shoulders are raised, and the teeth and hands clench. The skin can sweat and emptying the bladder becomes an urgent need.

Symptoms of heart thumping, sweating and breathlessness are seen in panic attacks as well as in fears and phobias. Fears and phobias can be acute realities in the lives of some older people – for example some are terrified of being burgled, (especially when an unusual sound is heard) or if they go out they are fearful of being attacked. Others may have phobias that their home will be taken from them. In more chronic situations, such symptoms may not be visible, but there is a low level of arousal, with an increase in adrenaline which, if persistent, can cause harm

Managing stress well plays a large part in the level of wellbeing we experience. It is not the frequency or intensity of stress that is the most significant; it is our ability to cope with it that makes the difference. This second stage in coping is important since it enables us to recognise and be alert to the signs and symptoms which show us that stress is there. It then requires us to take responsibility for doing something about it. Signs and symptoms differ – the important thing is to know our own.

Ways of managing stress

Being able to name our stresses, as well as knowing their signs and symptoms, leads to the third and final stage of developing ways of coping with it. This requires understanding, determination and practice. It means taking personal responsibility for our mental health. Coping, managing stress, is not just about surviving, but is concerned with living positively. Each of us has to manage our own coping; it is not something that can be done by others, no matter how supportive they may be.

Some people appear to cope better than others; everyone copes better at certain times, no one copes all the time.

Managing stress has to be learnt, and taking control of our lives and the various happenings that unfold is the key. An attitude of trying to manage our stresses, rather than letting them take control is the first step. Stress worsens when people feel helpless and feel they have no control over an issue, incident or relationship. This is never in fact true, as there is always something that can be done to reduce the stress effect. At times this will involve being pro-active, making things happen rather than always letting things happen. Learning from past experiences of success or failure can help us to see what we can do for ourselves, as well as when it might be preferable to get outside help.

There are some people who hold onto their stresses and become martyrs, in a way similar to some who hold onto their mental or physical illnesses because they cannot face life 'well'. Acting like a martyr can unconsciously be a way of getting attention, but it is a sad diminishing way to live.

Before examining specific coping strategies it is essential to stand back and see if the source of the stress can be removed or lessened in some way. This may not be possible for example in situations where a terminal illness is diagnosed or maybe a grandchild is born with a congenital disability. In these instances perceptions and attitudes have to change and this takes time as altered meanings and a deepening of insight develop. Most situations, however, can be changed, even radically. Major changes like moving out of home; or much smaller things may require alteration, like changing timetables, home rituals or ways of doing things. People may often complain about things without considering what can be done to ease matters, even in some small way, or going to others who could do something to lessen the stress.

There are often many ways of getting around a problem. For example if you can no longer drive a car that does not have to mean that you become housebound. Even if public transport is no longer usable or does not exist, taking a taxi, lifts from friends, neighbours or voluntary organisations are all possibilities. A taxi fund could be set up from the benefits of no longer having to pay money for car tax, NCT, insurance or petrol; quite a nest egg could accrue. It is sad to see people complaining and yet doing nothing about the problem.

Everyone has to discover for themselves effective ways of coping with stress that work for them, and put these into practice. Below are set out psychological strategies, and nine more specific physical approaches that are helpful.

1. *Psychological ways that help in managing stress*

❋ The first and most important is *learning the ability to live reflectively*. This means allowing time and space to know what is happening in our inner world. It enables us to become sensitive to early signs of stress, and as to whether personal needs are being adequately met. Growth in self-knowledge is a great asset in life. In order to tune in daily to our internal radio and hear what it is saying, certain steps have to be taken. Ideally, everyone should set aside some personal time for oneself each day. Many find this difficult, so starting with short five-minute periods or less could prove beneficial.

✳ *Admitting that stress is there* is an obvious step towards coping with it. As with alcoholics, nothing can be done until the problem is admitted and its reality faced. Depending on an individual's previous history and experiences, there may be the expectation on the part of others that a particular person has been and is good at coping. Inevitably, some of the stresses of the older years are different and hence have not been previously encountered. Admitting to stress is not admitting to failure. In fact, it could show strength of character and a sense of realism.

✳ *Talking the matter over with someone,* whether a partner, relative, friend or professional, is a well-recognised way of helping. It requires more than just talking 'about' the issue. It is helpful if, during the conversation, we come to discover and name as specifically as possible exactly what the problem is, and also to name the feeling that is present as a result of the stress. For instance, if one is deeply hurt, then say that, and don't soften it by saying you were 'a bit put out'. If one is in the listener role, it is all about listening, and not giving advice. At a later stage it might be helpful to indicate impartially other courses of action. Developing good support systems in life, such as friendships, is desirable for everyone so that there is someone to turn to in crisis moments. It is also helpful if we are aware of possible low points or moments, such as seasons of the year or anniversaries, and seek out supports around such times.

✳ *Trying to be objective* about what has actually happened to cause the stress, whether it arises from an event or a relationship, is not easy. When we are calm, it is useful to try and stand back and view the problem as if we were standing in someone else's shoes. When as objective a stance as is possible is reached, then there is need to face what has happened and see what requires changing and what has to be accepted. There is a tendency, when under stress, either to blame others or to blame oneself. Staying in the blaming place does not help us to cope; trying to be objective in order to gain insight into the reality of what has happened does.

✳ *Being open to seeing things differently* follows from the above. We need to challenge ourselves to see if our personal views and interpretations are correct. Questions like 'Am I being too rigid, too narrow in my thinking?' or 'Am I prejudiced?' can be helpful. Watching the use of certain words like 'must', 'should', 'ought', can be indicative. Often people use these words of themselves or others, for example, 'I must do this' or 'He should do that'. Such statements need to be challenged by further questions, 'Why must I do this?' or 'Why should he have to do that?' The only 'must' in life is not to harm ourselves or others; everything else is relative. It is desirable that we do many things in life, but they are not absolute imperatives.

❊ *Aiming not to give in to negative thinking* is vital. Negative thoughts are likely to come when we are under stress, but the important thing is not to 'nurse' these, but instead to try and move as quickly as possible from the 'poor me', 'why me' place. Watching our inner conversation is useful. Often our self-talk is negative, especially if we are low. Phrases like 'I'm no good, no one really cares about me, I'm too old, no one is interested in my opinions anymore' can surface. If we feed on negative thoughts, that can lead to expecting unpleasant things to happen and so the stress level gets worse.

❊ *Trying to take a positive approach,* and beginning by taking one small step, loosens the grip of the negative. Beginning with a shift towards positive self-talk helps: 'I'm OK', 'I'm OK despite my inadequacies, uncertainties',

'I value my opinions and the wisdom I have gained over the years'. The problem on hand may be difficult and the way forward unclear, but it is important to start somewhere and to begin by taking one small step. Doing nothing is not an option in managing stress.

❋ *Setting goals and making action plans* is a practical way to cope with stress. There are always alternative ways of looking at and doing things, so examining options and setting priorities, and having the courage to try out new things, are steps that need to be taken. The decisions to be specific and to have a precise time-scale built into them. For example 'I will have my main meal in the middle of the day starting next Monday'. 'I will go and see the solicitor about my will this week'. 'Tomorrow I will phone the hairdresser for an appointment on Friday morning.'

❋ *Searching out relevant information* to deepen understanding can considerably reduce stress. Not knowing, not having sufficient information about something raises anxiety levels which can add to the existing stress. Often when the truth is known, even if it brings bad news, it can also bring a sense of relief, since there is no longer the feeling of being in the dark. Fear of the unknown, especially if something sinister is anticipated, is always stressful, so again information regarding knowing what to expect in particular circumstances can considerably reduce stress.

❄ *Looking for something positive* is always helpful. In acute stress this may be difficult, but where there is chronic stress this can be very beneficial. People speak of the new friends they made in and through their difficulties, of the things they have learnt about themselves, of how their values have changed for the better, of how they have gained an insight into suffering that they would otherwise never have known.

❄ *Learning the art of saying goodbye* is often necessary in the stresses of life. What is required may involve a letting go of people, pets, places, tasks or roles. The process of letting go and moving on is painful. However, it is only by entering into the pain and going through it that we discover this is the way out of the stress. As noted earlier in this book, letting go and saying goodbye involves loss and it is important to grieve adequately over the losses so that we can move on.

❄ *Setting realistic goals* plays a large part in both preventing and coping with the stresses ingrained in the ordinary everyday happenings of life.

First of all, there are the goals we set for ourselves. We can set goals that are unrealistically high, as may happen with a perfectionist. When personal expectations are too high, and they are not achieved, negative feelings are aroused. People become despondent, worry and then feel guilty because they do not achieve or do as much as they think they ought. What is demanded of each of us is to do what is reasonably possible. And even if we do fall short of what is reasonable, the managing of such a failure can become something positive.

Secondly, we can allow others to make unrealistic demands on us, expecting us to be or act in certain ways. This can happen in all relationships and especially in close ones. It is important not to take these unrealistic expectations on board. We need to know our limits and not to allow ourselves to become over-stretched by another person.

Finally, setting goals for others can also cause stress. Parents for example, can sometimes do this with their children. Apart from being unhelpful for the son or daughter, it is also unhelpful to the parent who will have to cope with feelings of disappointment, of being let down. Such feelings can last for years, causing persistent stress.

2. *Physical ways that help in managing stress*

❋ *Enjoyment* is a great stress reducer. Life can become overly serious so there is need to counteract this at times by developing a 'playful' element. Enjoyment is an essential component to living fully. It is never too late to learn this important dimension of living. It is especially necessary not to allow ourselves become so low and despondent that we can no longer enjoy anything. Enjoyment is often not connected with the exotic, but rather the simple things of life, like a walk or talking to a friend.

❈ *Leisure activities* are something we enjoy doing, but they are done on a regular basis and so some discipline is necessary in such activities on the days we do not feel like participating. Adherence to a leisure activity can both prevent and considerably lessen the stresses of life.

❈ *Moving out of the environment* is sometimes indicated as part of stress management. In an emergency situation, for instance after a serious quarrel, or at a deadline moment and one's computer breaks down, it can be useful to escape for a while in order to cool off and stand back from what has happened. A day's outing, a weekend away, holidays, are all beneficial in times of stress. Everything tends to be seen differently after a break away from our normal environment.

❈ *Doing one thing at a time* without rushing enables us to get into the present moment. Being at what we are at in a particular moment of time can be very therapeutic. This is specially necessary during times of acute stress when it is difficult to settle down to anything, For example, to say 'now I am going to make a cup of tea' and do just that.

❈ *Putting energy into things we like doing and do well* is valuable with acute forms of stress. Such moments are not the time to tackle difficult and unpleasant tasks. It is also not the time to put ourselves in circumstances where over-reaction is possible. For example, if a person has recently been bereaved or separated, social events in the early days following such events need to be chosen with thought.

✳ *Knowing and holding onto 'anchor points'* helps in both acute and chronic stress. For example, these could be places (a favourite spot), relationships that we enjoy (especially those that restore confidence and bring life), gardening, going to a film, a walk in the park...

✳ *Doing something for someone else* can be a good stress reducer. This might seem strange for someone who is incapacitated by illness or disability, yet it is true for everyone. The doing of a task, like visiting someone, or making a phone call, or even reaching out in concerned thought to someone helps restore a sense of perspective about our own difficulties.

✳ *Looking after our own general health* is required by everyone but this is particularly necessary during periods of stress. Adequate rest, exercise and diet must be attended to with more care. If our physical health is in reasonable order this will enhance a sense of wellbeing which in turn enables us to cope better with stress

✳ *Relaxation exercises* are often the first thing that comes to people's minds when stress is spoken about. While coping with stress demands much more than just being able to relax, relaxation exercises are helpful to many people.

There are a large number of techniques available but all include certain basics, which are as follows:

Take up a comfortable, well-supported posture, ideally lying down or well supported in a chair with arms.

Set a quiet atmosphere, without too much light, and with sufficient heat.

Give sufficient time, 20 minutes minimum, to arrive at a reasonable level of relaxation. There is no such thing as instant relaxation.

Close one's eyes, just listen to your breathing. Do not change the rhythm, just listen to it and go with it. This can be done for most, or all, of the exercise.

Other techniques can be added but are not essential. Examples include: using a mantra or focusing on an object, such as a lighted candle or flower.

CHAPTER 6

The Satisfactions of the Older Years

"There is only one art and that is the art of living." These striking words come from poet W.B. Yeats. Living is indeed an art, the art form which is perfected and receives its final touches in our older years. The tapestry of our life may take on unexpected designs and blending of colours if the later decades are lived in a spirit of adventure, creativity and heightened awareness. While, for some, these years may have moments of exuberance and ecstasy, for many it is more likely to be a time of quieter discoveries, where "there lives the dearest freshest deep down things", spoken of by Gerard Manley Hopkins. It is a time of opportunity for re-awakening the fresh child-like wonder of discovering truth and beauty, in ways that up to now were only glimpsed at.

Chapter Three discussed the question of answering human needs in a reasonable and integrated manner. These needs can be further divided into those elementary ones which are necessary for living, and those needs which enable one to flourish as a human person, as the unique individual that I am. Our older years allow us to taste this experience of flourishing in new and richer ways than in previous years where often such experiences were transient. This sense of fulfilment will not be as present to those who suffer from depression, but this is not to deny that the possibility is open to everyone, especially if we expect it and do what we can to facilitate it happening.

When younger, or in the middle years, most people get caught up in earning a living, developing a career, raising a family. With such responsibilities now in the main over, there is the possibility of concentrating more fully on the art of living in a more conscious way. It is not a question of doing a whole lot of things for this to happen (although it could include that), but rather it is a case of experiencing, savouring more deeply whatever we do. So much of life is inevitably lived at a superficial level, but now the challenge is to greater quality in our being and doing, as opposed to sheer quantity. Inherent in this new perspective is a movement from a life of complexity towards one of a rich simplicity. The best experiences, as we continue on our maturing journey, are likely to be the simple ones like a good conversation with a friend, examining a leaf, listening to the sound of children at play, taking the dog for a walk, luxuriating in a bath and reading afresh a favourite poem or novel.

The experience of satisfaction in our older years contains within it the knowledge that our present experience of living is in the main what we want it to be. It might not be what we earlier envisaged it might be, yet the reality of life as it is now can truly be described as personally satisfying. Satisfaction, like other qualities connected with human living, is a relative concept, and is experienced in varying degrees of intensity. It is always open to constant fluctuations. Satisfaction in life implies a sense of contentment, which, while never complete, is an experience that can be named as our normal state of being. Anxieties, fears, and all the other range of negative emotions will come and go, but the predominant one that remains is that of satisfaction or contentment.

There is a growing awareness, particularly among health care professionals and researchers, of the importance of quality of life (QoL) as an important evaluation of health status both pre and post medical interventions. There is no agreement as to how quality of life can be measured precisely because it is based on an individual's personal assessment of life experience. Since it is by its very nature a self-report, it defies external set measurements. Attempts have been made in the past to try out such measurements and one factor came through, namely that older respondents were in general happier with their lives than the younger group. Younger people may pity older people, not realising that many older people are getting more out of life than they are themselves.

The QoL assessment has also been used in evaluating the outcome of elective surgical procedures like joint replacement and coronary artery by-pass grafts. Apart from measuring the technical success of the operation the quality of life of the person after the operation was also taken into account. Life satisfaction scales can be reasonably high, even in older people who have serious health problems. A survey done several years ago in Wales showed that a group aged 75-95 years felt that their health was good, at least 'alright' for their age, even though three quarters of this group had some physical limitations.

The experience of satisfaction, like happiness, cannot be attained *per se*. It is the by-product or result of our attitudes, values and lifestyles. Satisfaction can, however, be facilitated by certain measures and three in particular will be mentioned here. Other ways have been discussed in chapter two on retirement. The areas treated here are: Remaining a contributor to society in some way, no matter how small, living a life of greater awareness through a heightened use of our senses; and a greater exposure to nature and the world of the arts.

Remaining a contributor to society

Remaining a giver has been previously touched on, but it cannot be over emphasised. A key satisfaction in living for all age groups lies in concern for others and especially those in need. We remain 'our brother's keeper' throughout life; this inevitable means we try to remain aware of the needs of others as well as our own. A failure to remain compassionate can make our world become very small. The joy in giving, in being able to love people and our world, remains the core of fulfilled living. If we deny ourselves this side of living, our lives can become empty, because a prime ingredient to fulfilled living is missing. In addition to needing the support of others as we age, there is also the need in turn to be a supporter, at least emotionally, of those who are close to us, as well as being an encourager. Offering a smile or a word of gratitude is likely to be much appreciated by those who may be caring for us. The actual ways we reach out to others are unique to each one, but the need to both give and receive love is fundamental to every human person.

Living a life of awareness through a heightened use of our senses

All of us live limited lives. We never develop our potential anywhere near what is possible, largely due to our lack of awareness. Fulfilled living is about living with greater awareness and this is closely linked with both our outer and inner senses. Our outer and inner senses are also closely connected with each other – seeing with insight; hearing with inner listening; touching with sensitivity; tasting with inner relishing, such as relishing life itself; smelling with inner savouring of intangible realities like picking up atmosphere in a gathering, or in one's surroundings.

A strange paradox is noticeable in our older years, namely that as our senses diminish in physiological acuteness, our appreciation and wonder at such gifts and endowments often grow. The senses are the pinnacle of all our bodily functions, powers, abilities. They are the way through which we learn all we know. They are also the way through which we communicate with each other and the world. If we are totally deprived of one or more of these senses, we are truly deprived of enormous sources of enrichment. The senses are *par excellence* the gateway to full living, and the older years provide time and opportunity to enter this gate, and to appreciate and enjoy the marvels that are to be found in every human situation. Earlier in life we may have been too functional and simply taken our senses for granted and so missed many things, simply because we did not discover the enrichment of really looking, hearing, smelling, touching and tasting. Moving from mind to sense helps restore this often largely lost dimension to living. For those who want it, the older years can be a time for developing our perceptual self, our powers of perceiving reality, what is really real around us. Doing this can lead to an experience similar to that of Howard Carter when he peered into the tomb of Tutankhamun (which had be closed for 4,000 years). He exclaimed the striking words: "I see marvellous things." Sense living helps us to de-familiarise the familiar, which is always rich for those whose sense life is open to the macro and micro world both around us and within. Patrick Kavanagh says succinctly as only a poet can: "Ordinary things have lovely wings."

Developing our sense-life calls us to certain behaviours and attitudes. The *first* of these is time and the ability to stop rushing. More positively, it means making time 'to stand and stare' so that we can really hear, touch, taste and smell. *Secondly,* it calls for an outlook that is awake, one that is ready for surprises and the unexpected, and a willingness to drop plans in order to capture and savour the moment – the happening that presents itself for full attention. *Thirdly,* it requires watching our fatigue levels, since tiredness dulls awareness and thus it means taking adequate periods of rest. *Fourthly,* it means appreciating and caring adequately for our sense organs, eyes, ears, taste buds, skin, nose – and related aids – spectacles, hearing aids, dentures. *Finally,* our senses are aroused by stimulation and those senses whose function is becoming diminished may need the assistance of increased stimulation. For example, our sense of smell can weaken, *so* deliberately setting out to smell particularly pleasant and pungent scents, can be helpful in keeping this sense alive and even reawakening it to what previously went unnoticed. The same can be done for taste by adding different or slightly strong flavours to food.

Our outer senses, as already said, are linked with a set of inner senses. Coming to our senses can arouse in us a sense of wonder, awe and delight at what is without as well as what lies within. When we *see* colour, shape, size, form – for example, a sunset, the fingers of a newborn child, a work of art – we expand our insight into truth and beauty. When we really *hear* sounds – bird song, music, the human voice – in all their rich variety of tone, volume and texture, we enlarge our powers of inner listening to the spoken and unspoken, to the inner and outer voices, to the riches of silence as well as sound. When we *taste* food or drink and its texture and flavours, we learn inner relishing, that capacity to delight in things, people, places, events, truth and beauty. When we *smell* both the pleasant and unpleasant we arouse in ourselves an inner awareness of the ephemeral or intangible, such as becoming sensitive to an atmosphere in a situation, or experiencing the power of association that links us to the past, as well as the exotic. When we *touch,* we discover hardness or softness, shape, texture, temperature, and are awakened to similar inner qualities in ourselves and others. Touch, possibly the most sacred sense of all because of its power to communicate intimacy, is the sense organ that is left intact in most people until their death. We freely touch the small baby, and instinctively most people feel free to touch the dying person. Sadly, some people are inhibited in their use and receiving of touch, and hence miss the richness inherent in this particular sense.

Touch and all our senses are given to be used fully, freely and appropriately. They help to protect by, for example, alerting us to danger, but pre-eminently they are there for communication, appreciation and enjoyment. The greatest adventure of our older years may be found in the unfathomable riches discovered in the simple opening of ourselves, through our senses, to the wonder of the universe. There is a sense of wonderment too when we can appreciate our own being. This was so strong for the psalmist that he exclaimed: "For the wonder of my being I thank you."

Exposure to the world of the arts

The satisfactions of the older years can be greatly enhanced by exposure to the arts – an exposure of depth rather than quantity. Many of us, especially in the west, have had a variety of experiences and the sheer variety fosters a certain superficiality. How many books or films can we really recall? - probably only the few whose impact we were open to and which said something particularly significant to us. The older years are a time to select and savour what really attracts us in the line of music, poetry, drama, painting, sculpture, literature, dance and other art forms. Whether the material is new to us, or we are returning to the familiar, is immaterial. What matters is that our experience is one that is personally enriching, delight-filled and possibly challenging. Such activity lends itself to stretching our imagination which may have been suppressed in earlier times by the humdrum of life. A fresh releasing of our imaginative powers can prove very freeing. It can also reveal a creative side to oneself, even possibly to becoming an inventor!

The art experience has two forms of expression – we can develop our appreciation of art, or enter into the creation of art ourselves. For example we can read, or try writing; view paintings, or paint; listen to music or compose. Re-entering or trying dance or free movement for the first time, even in our eighties can be truly liberating and can help to integrate growth in inner freedom with body freedom. The act of creating, whether dancing, designing a garden, sculpting or whatever, can be one of life's most satisfying experiences. It is fortunately not uncommon for older people to discover for the first time talents they never knew existed, or build on talents which up to now had largely lain dormant. A quotation from Pablo Casals, the great Spanish musician reinforces all that has been said: "On my last birthday I was 93. This is not young of course... but age is a relative matter. If you continue to work and absorb the beauty of the world about you, you find that age does not necessarily mean getting old. I feel many things more intensely than before and for me life grows more fascinating... The man who works is never bored, is never old. Work and interest in worthwhile things are the best remedy for age. Each day I am reborn. Each day I must begin again."

This remarkable approach to life of someone at 93 echoes well the words of the Old Testament prophet Isaiah written in the 7th century BC: "Now I am revealing new things to you, things hidden and unknown to you, created just now, this very moment, of these things you have heard nothing until now, so that you cannot say, 'O yes, I knew all this.'"

In the last decades of life, many do develop fresh and absorbing interests, fall in love and in general discover excitement and newness in an endless number of ways. Browning has the lovely lines: "Grow old along with me; for the best is yet to come."

CHAPTER SEVEN

Ageing in Wisdom, Hope and Joy

This chapter attempts to bring together many of the strands related to ageing already referred to in this book while focusing in a special way on the experiencing of wisdom, hope and joy in our older years. We have only one life cycle to live and, as we grow older, the realisation comes that it is the actual living of life that is the source of our wisdom, hope and joy. As we move on towards fulfilling the cycle of our lives, what is experienced as true and authentic assumes greater relevance and importance. No book on ageing would be compete if it did not endeavour to explore wisdom, and joy, which can and often do emerge as important values in the latter part of life.

Ageing is a process of growth, which as it unfolds, can slowly reveal to us the great mystery that life is for all of us. The journey of living is normally towards simplicity and hopefully to a greater capacity to give, until ultimately the call for all is the giving up of our own lives in the form we know it. Older people who live fully are great prophets who can enable those less mature to enter more deeply into the mystery of living. Fulfilled ageing allows us to discover more and more life's treasures and, *par excellence*, the wonder of what it is to be a unique and fully alive human being. Ageing is therefore a time for hope, not despair; for maturing in wisdom, not for personal diminishment; a time for enjoyment, not for colourless living.

❁   WISDOM

The Wisdom literature of the Old Testament, written over 2,000 years ago, is full of gems about the nature and qualities of wisdom, such as: "Wisdom is bright and does not grow dim. By those who love her she is readily seen and found by those who look for her." The wisdom spoken of is very much the wisdom of the heart so that wisdom and love are closely related; indeed mature love's flower is wisdom. One often hears: 'He/ she has matured with the years.' It is the mellowing of the person especially shown in their ability to love well, with integrity and generosity, that makes a person wise. Mature love is likened to a rich red wine; it is a love which grows in depth and perspective, being refined in the furnace of the cycle of one's own life lived fully.

Another well-known Wisdom passage says:

There is a season for everything:
A time for giving birth, a time for dying;
A time for planting, a time for uprooting what has
been planted;
A time for knocking down, a time for building;
A time for tears, a time for laughter;
A time for mourning, a time for dancing...;
A time for keeping, a time for throwing away;
A time for keeping silent, a time for speaking;
A time for war, a time for peace.

The older years are a time for all these things, and it is above all the wisdom of love that discerns the truth of what each moment offers. Wisdom is considered one of the special fruits of the older years; years which allows us to live with a certain harmony and contentedness amidst the many complexities of life. Part of wisdom's gift is its power to play with opposites, to establish a synthesis as opposed to compromise.

The later decades of life are a time to let go of many things, and one is the world of compromise, to finding more and more a synthesis and integration in our lives. The ability to live in greater simplicity and serenity in the midst of paradox and complexity, is the fruit of wisdom. Wisdom can be found in the young as well as the old, but it is more likely to emerge as a person matures with age. Wisdom flows from growth in our personal experience of what it is to be truly human, and our older years are a special time to complete this task of discovering what being human is truly about.

One way of dividing the human journey is to view it in four stages. The first decade is all about the child exploring what it is to be a human being. The second stage, which can cover many decades, is about discovering our individuality and this includes within it the desire to achieve, to be significant in some way, shown by the various positions we adopt within society. The third stage, which often emerges in the later middle or earlier older years, can carry a note of a more serious spiritual quest, where there is a movement from achievement to that of finding meaning; the fourth and final stage is about an enriched experience of the first stage, namely about living more fully our own unique human self.

The fourth stage partly emerges from a growing awareness of our own vulnerabilities. As Jung would say, it is about getting in touch with our 'shadow', the darker side of ourselves, while at the same time being in tune with our inner strengths. Discovering the opposites in oneself and developing 'the power to play with' these, helps to form an integrated self and this is part of the growth process of our older years. It is linked with the search for meaning and fulfilment which is an essential component of a person who remains a searcher for truth. Einstein says: "The person who regards his life as meaningless, is not merely unhappy but hardly fit to live." The search for what life is about affects us all through life, becoming more pressing at certain times and particularly in moments of crisis. This search can be very acute for young people but also for older people. There are those who have the backdrop of a religious sense, or who re-discover or even discover for the first time a deep-down faith that they can rely on to make sense of their lives. Religious faith is more likely to sustain and console those who depend not so much on belief systems but rather on the gift of faith itself; a faith in God 'in whom we live, move and have our being'. Faith is a loving knowledge born of religious love. Pascal describes faith in terms of the heart having reasons which reason does not know. Authentic religious experience can bring an awareness of being touched in some way by divine mystery, a mystery of love and awe that can fill its receivers with peace, love and freedom.

The search for what life is about effects everyone but sadly some appear to fail to discover meaning and particularly those who suffer from severe depression. Seeing the point to life can, for some, become a real issue and tempt a person to try or actually commit suicide (and this can happen in all age groups in society).

Wisdom also includes being in touch not only with our own evolving sense of what it is to be human, but also involves the ability to stay in touch with the humanity of others – both those close to us and humankind in general. This is what compassion is all about. This means being able to rejoice with all the happenings we know to be good, while allowing ourselves to be disturbed by the inhumanity we find in both ourselves and others. Growth in awareness also includes being in touch with the concerns of the created world and doing our bit to foster nature's ecological balance.

Wisdom comes to people in innumerable ways. We associate this gift with artists, mystics, philosophers, gurus, while at the same time it has always been recognised that it can be found among simple people who have had no formal education. Largely, wisdom emerges from people who are reflective – reflective about what lies deep within themselves as well as living with a reflective awareness of all that is outside the self, including people, ideas, issues, creation and art. At certain moments in the older years, people are likely to take stock of themselves and look back over life. Part of this process is to own our own history, which is largely influenced by the many choices we have made throughout life. Endo, the Japanese novelist says: "Just as with all interpersonal relationships in our life we are made to suffer by those things we have chosen, it is in confronting our choices we gradually discover ourselves." The discovery of self is always ongoing and very much part of growth in wisdom. We are never static, and maybe it is in our older years that the most major changes, as well as major discoveries, are made. The human spirit has unfathomable capacity for truth, beauty, freedom and love. The person who remains open to reality in life, despite their possible diminished functional ability and increasing fatigue, can remain open to absorb and experience the new in ways that are both painful and enriching. Growth always involves pain as well as enrichment. If the mind remains alert and a spirit of awareness is fostered, the inner spirit can remain very much alive. Trusting in the truth which our own heart dictates, we continue to learn, as the Book of Wisdom reminds us: "In the secret of my heart teach me wisdom."

❀ HOPE

Hope can be summed up well in the words of the 14th century mystic, Julian of Norwich: "All shall be well, and all shall be well, and you shall perceive how all manner of things shall be well." Hope is rooted in reality and so it is not to be associated with mere fantasy or an unreal sense of optimism. Neither is hope realised in the mere fulfilment of wishes. It is something deeper and more open-ended. Hope provides an outlook which trusts in the possibilities that are open to those who endeavour to live their human existence to the full. Disappointments will occur, but hope does not allow these to take hold. In fact, it is often through coping with disappointments that a hopeful person discovers the possibility of new openings and wider horizons opening up to them. Hope challenges to what lies further, to what is beyond our normal range of inner vision. It stretches us to both the beyond as well as to the greater depths that exist in the present. There is always more to each moment than we have the capacity to hold/experience, but growth in hope liberates us to develop further our potential to a far wider and deeper range of experiences. Hope is closely linked with courage and an explorer spirit.

An essential dimension of hope is that it does not allow a sense of ultimate disappointment or helplessness to permeate the inner core of our being. True hope, too, helps to ease away the pain of remorse, bitterness and regret. While hope admits these and other feelings, hope has the power to filter through and allow new vistas to open up, particularly as we start to let go of that which is diminishing us. Hope also allows for a change in priorities to take place, where what is experienced as personally enriching, rather than the 'oughts' in life, takes greater precedence. It is never too late to "fall in love with life", as Shirley Valentine so well articulated.

Hope is very much connected with vision – a vision which includes within it the notion 'that the best is still to come'. When we no longer cling to our illusions, vision, perspective and insight flourish. Hope is closely linked with enlightenment which is connected with these latter three qualities. Illumination can come in flash, but more normally comes slowly or in stages. Illumination can lead to changed meanings, changed perspectives, even to a changed notion about time. Hope is about letting go of anxiety, and especially excessive anxiety regarding the future, while at the same time it does not avoid planning in a reasonable manner for the years ahead.

Even the experience of darkness, fatigue, or depression does not quench hope, or at least need not. Living with the knowledge that things pass and that the power of hope is there to sustain us in such circumstances gives, even if only dimly, the ability to live with the expectancy of something greater to come. Darkness can overwhelm us, particularly if we shut out the many signs of light which both surround us and lie deep within ourselves. The darkness of the older years found in much thinking and literature on ageing (including discussions on euthanasia) is partly due to a failure to see the light that is available to all who wish to discover the 'now' opportunities of our individual life situations.

Hope is both a gift and a quality which emerges from the actual living of life. It is often linked with endurance, the ability to hang in, even when the going is difficult. But when we can do this, as Paul of Tarsus reminds us, 'hope does not disappoint us'. Those with religious faith and those who have none are blessed if they remain open to the future, aware that life has always something more, something new to offer us. Someone who lives with hope will not find life dull, drab or boring. Each day offers fresh opportunities, fresh surprises. Mostly these will not be dramatic, but are there to be savoured in all their simplicity and ordinariness.

When we grow to accept ourselves for who we are, and not link our value to past achievements or what we can or cannot do in the now, then we, like the tree, reach maturity. The power of hope which allows us to trust in ourselves and others is what brings life. The expanding visions which grow through hope, even as the ageing process takes its toll, enable us to see beyond limitations. It invites us to surrender to life as it is now, and it is where "the distinction between life and death loses its pain" (H. Nouwen).

Hope is linked with desires. We have surface desires which are not always in tune with the truth of who we are. Discernment is needed to discover our deep-down desires, some of which we may need to re-articulate and allow surface again for hope to come to fulfilment. Desires and dreams are related to one another. Unfulfilled dreams of earlier years can sometimes find realisation in unexpected ways, if opportunities are explored and connections made between the dream and the real world. Hope too gives the courage which allows us to earth our dreams. All this becomes possible if we listen to what our dreams are saying to us. Allowing the attempts of others to dampen, diminish or even laugh at our hopes and dreams must be fought. Pope John XXIII was an outstanding example of an older person who allowed a Church council to take root, despite his knowing that he would be unlikely to see it through. This particular dream affected the lives of people for centuries to follow thus shaping history in a remarkable way.

Our attitude to death, our own in particular, will colour the level of hope experienced. Some people have a natural fear of death, although such a fear is often more about the process of dying rather than death itself. Fear is an emotion largely connected with the unknown, and death is the great unknown. Religious faith may help some people alleviate this fear, but fear of itself does not guarantee the elimination of the fear of death. It is important that the presence or absence of fear not be taken as a measure of a person's faith, either by themselves or others. Fear of death, like any other fear has to be gently faced and worked through and this may require the help of another person if its crippling effect is to be lessened. Erick Ericson remarked "that only in a society in which the old do not fear death, will the young be able not to fear life. Put another way, it could be stated that only in a society in which the old can find meaning in their lives, will the young have confidence in any meanings they may be offered."

Aldous Huxley gives great hope when he says to his dying wife: "Let go, let go... go forward into the light. Let yourself be carried into the light. No memories, no regrets, no looking backwards, no apprehensive thoughts about your own or anyone else's future. Only light." These words are echoed in similar fashion by a dying Dutch priest, Hans Fortman: "I proceed from the simple irrefutable fact that in the crucial moments of this life (such as death), even though people come from diverging cultures and religions, they find that same essential word: Light! For isn't it true? There must be a basic similarity between the Enlightenment spoken of by the Hindus and Buddhists and the Eternal Light of the Christians. Both die into the Light."

Light, enlightenment, is not only for those approaching death. It is a reality that can be progressively discovered in the ordinary things of our everyday, as well as in the extraordinary moments. Enlightenment is a fruit of hope which enables us to remain open to all that happens to us, and particularly as we continue our exploring work of completing both our outer and inner life's journey. T.S. Eliot explains this sentiment so well when he says: "Old men ought to be explorers, here or there does not matter. To a further intensity, a deeper communion ... in the end is our beginning."

✿ JOY

One of the best ways of opening people to profound human truths is through the power of a story and this particular section will both begin and end with one:

The Master was in an expansive mood so his disciples sought to learn from him the stages he had passed through in his quest for the divine. "God first led me by the hand," he said, "into the Land of Action and there I dwelt for several years. Then he returned and led me to the Land of Sorrows; there I lived until my heart was purged of every inordinate attachment. That is when I found myself in the Land of Love whose burning flames consumed whatever was left in me of self. This brought me to the Land of Silence where the mysteries of life and death were bared before my wondering eyes." "Was that the final stage of your quest?" they asked. "No" the Master said. "One day God said, 'Today I shall take you to the innermost sanctuary of the Temple, to the heart of God himself.' And I was lead to the Land of Laughter."

Joy is one of our primary emotions and is associated with a range of feeling experiences, from moments of ecstasy, passion, exhilaration, to a quieter form of inner contentment. Feelings of joy can surge at unexpected moments, or joy can be the normal inner state that pervades the life of an individual. Joy can manifest in various outward expressions, from smiles and laughter to dancing and even jumping for joy. Joy is mentioned several times in the Bible: "However great the number of years a man may live, let him enjoy them all. No enjoyment surpasses cheerful heart. Joy is what gives him length of days." (Wisdom) At the heart of the Gospel is the theme of joy, this central message being announced at the outset: "I bring you news of great joy" to which is added immediately, "a joy to be shared by all the people" (Luke).

Much discussion on ageing focuses on its difficulties, and little is said about its joys. It is something like the way bad news makes the headlines, while good news rarely does. Stereotyping ageing, especially seeing the older years in the light of the 20% of people who are frail mentally or physically, highlights the unattractive face of ageing in people's consciousness. While deep joy can and does exist in these 20% of people, it is abundantly open to the remaining 80% to experience much joy as they age.

Unlike wisdom, which can be sought, or hope, whose presence can be encouraged and fostered, joy is something that happens to us. We cannot seek it, in fact the more we consciously try to do so, the more it may elude us. It is a by-product of our attitudes and desires and the way we live our lives. Joy is more likely to emerge if we value life and note its preciousness in both the small and major happenings of ordinary everyday living, such as the smile of a baby, an unexpected meeting, the beauty of nature or an insight received. One of the greatest joys of many older people is being in the presence of their grand and great-grandchildren.

Joy is about delighting in, wondering at, being playful about, all that happens in the world around us, as well as what takes place within ourselves. Everything, including tragic moments, can in some way have a joy-filled dimension. One of the great joyous moments is undoubtedly for a mother at the birth of her child. She forgets the pain when the baby is born. Yet why is it that joy seems to evaporate, appear almost absent in the lives of many? Undoubtedly there is great suffering in the lives of numerous people across the world, due to extreme forms of poverty, wars, terrorist activities etc. We are indeed largely fortunate living in Europe where experiencing joy is not beyond reach. Yet it is also astonishingly true that contagious joy can be found among the poorest of the poor. While living without even basic food and water supplies, they yet have the freedom to capture the joy of the moment in a way that we in the West sometimes miss.

Joy is something which invades us – all we can do is predispose ourselves for it. Like falling asleep or falling in love, so we too fall into joy. Joy is more likely to come to those who try to live liberated lives; to those who consciously work at developing inner freedom. Living joyfully, in this sense, entails not clinging to things, people, or practices. This can lead to feelings of devastation when they are no longer available. This letting-go may include realities that have been very precious to us and ultimately includes the letting go of our own life. As a small child, Chaim Potok recalls asking his father why a bird should die, why death at all, and received the following answer: "so life would be precious. Something that is yours forever is never precious." Growth in awareness of the fragility of all that is, the transient nature of everything, greatly assists us in appreciating joyous moments as they come to us. Moments of intense joy, even rapture can last for mere seconds, but the remembrance of them can last a lifetime.

Joy is linked with humour, which has been described as knowledge with a soft smile. Humour is a great blessing to possess. It has the capacity to relativise without ridicule or becoming cynical. It enables us to take ourselves, others and life events seriously, but never too seriously. To be able to see the humorous side of things is all part of growth in understanding and thus is a valued way of coming closer to truth. So much in human living is relative – values, issues, people, even life itself. A great realisation that comes gradually over life is that nothing is absolute except love. "Love never ends" says a famous biblical phrase. In relation to love, everything else fades into insignificance.

A humorous person has the ability to discover fun almost anywhere. Such people are often very balanced since they have a healthy perspective on life and are generally good to be with. Humour and joy are often connected with playfulness, an activity so prominent and essential in the life of a child. Play leads to delight and often wonder, both of which result in joy. Play is not the same as a leisure activity. The latter can often be very serious and demanding. Play is spontaneous, it refreshes, it is an experience of fun and freedom and often has an outside-time quality about it. The laughter and smiles of children at play have an appealing, contagious quality. The laughter and smiles of older people can also be special. The joy that is found in younger and older people often carries a particular type of radiance so that their joy affects not only themselves but reaches out to touch others in a special way. Laughter, joy and play all help the serious world we live in to become more light-hearted. A heavy-hearted person has great difficulty in experiencing joy in living. Groucho Marx was someone who brought a sense of fun and light-heartedness to many people by his playful pranks on film. He seems to have experienced joy himself: "Each morning I open my eyes I say to myself; I, not events have the power to make me happy today. I can choose which it shall be. Yesterday is dead, tomorrow hasn't arrived yet. I have just one day, today, and I'm going to be happy in it."

Joy can be something bubbly or it can manifest itself in serenity and contentment. The latter state of living is likely to be the consequence of our approach to life, which does not allow circumstances and events, even if traumatic, to upset us unduly. Upset clouds perception and only adds to the trauma. Fortunately, we now live in an age where medicine, in particular good drug therapy and other helps, can eliminate or keep to a minimum physical pain. The causes of emotional and spiritual pain come from our reactions to the varying circumstances of our lives and especially according to Ireland's first palliative care consultant, Michael Kearney, when "our behaviour and general lifestyle are not in harmony with our deepest desires".

Someone who knows the world of joy is more likely to be earthed in the real world and live in the present. Even if that present proves difficult, it is rarely intolerable. Life can have its harsh, unbearable moments at times, but rarely do events, no matter how extreme the pain that surrounds them, have the power to take away our joy unless we allow them to do so. Finding ourselves on the 'poor me' place can arouse very negative feelings and needs to be counteracted as soon as we are aware of such an occurrence. Each happening in life is open to being joy-filled at a deep level, and responsible living is about not being pulled down by upset feelings, which often are surface and will pass, especially if we manage them constructively. Dietrich Bonhoeffer writes movingly from prison in his last letter to his fiancé just before his execution: 'I have not felt lonely or abandoned for one moment. You must not think that I am unhappy. What is happiness and what is unhappiness? It depends so little on the circumstances. It depends really on that which happens inside a person. I am grateful every day that I have you and that makes me happy.'

Anthony de Mello calls us "to wake up" to life, to "rediscover life". Certainly this is the path to follow if we wish to experience our older years as fulfilling. We cannot acquire joy, as he points out, since we already have it. What happens is that we block it from surfacing in our lives. Hence our task is to remove the blocks and allow joy's existence to flourish. He quotes an Eastern saying: "When the eye is unobstructed, the result is sight; when the mind is unobstructed, the result is truth; when the heart is unobstructed the result is joy and love." What we tend to see and name as our sources of joy can often be the very things that bind us and thus hinder us from experiencing true joy. For example, if our hearts are too attached to wealth, possessions, relationships, health or 'enjoyments', such things can result in a lack of joy. Fear of losing, or actual loss of these possessions can take hold of us and prevent real joy surfacing. If actual loss does occur, a sense of devastation can ensue. There is so much in life that can give joy, but if we over-focus on particular people, places, possessions as the source of our joy, and when one of these is no longer there for us, or is not there in the way we would like it to be, then we can become sad, upset, frustrated and lacking in joy. Another Eastern quotation aptly says: "When you enjoy the scent of a thousand flowers, you are not going to feel too bad at the lack of one." In other words, our joy does not depend on any one person or thing – Mary or

George, our possessions, ideas, talents or good health. Our heart is inevitably drawn to where our treasure is. If our treasure lies solely in one person or particular possessions, it will be tied there. If our treasure is in freedom, love, beauty, truth, then the heart which is tied to these has an endless source of joy available. This does not mean that we do not have possessions or value our relationships, but it does mean that they are not our sole treasure in life.

It is very difficult to define joy for ourselves, and one of the reasons is that it is hard to experience true joy until we begin to drop our attachments. Everyone recognises moments of joy when they happen, and such moments are likely to have a fleeting quality about them. A particular characteristic of joyous moments is that they are unexpected, unique, carry their own special flavour, and are largely unrepeatable. Joy is not to be confused with thrills or pleasure. Joy is something which deeply satisfies the human heart, since it is something which affects the core of our spirit. In its most profound sense, joy is about the experience of bliss. Such an experience is open to everyone and a step in the direction of tasting such an experience is to believe in its possibility.

As we grow in freedom and non-attachment, we are left with more energy and enthusiasm for living. We are also likely to become more empowering and creative people. Allowing ourselves to be surprised by the happenings in our personal lives is a way to facilitate the emergence of joy. C.S. Lewis titled his autobiography *Surprised by Joy*. Soon after it was finished, he was entirely surprised by one of the greatest joys of his life – a Joy in person and in name, who later became his wife!

This section will end with another eastern story, entitled *The Diamond,* which illustrates a source where true and abundant joy is found:

The wise man had reached the outskirts of the village and settled down under a tree for the night, when a villager came running up to him and said, "The stone! The stone! Give me the precious stone." "What stone?" asked the wise man. "Last night the Lord Shiva appeared to me in a dream," said the villager, "and told me that if I went to the outskirts of the village at dusk I should find a wise man who would give me a precious stone that would make me rich forever." The wise man rummaged in his bag and pulled out the stone. "He probably meant this one," he said, as he handed the stone over to the villager. "I found it in a forest path some days ago. You can certainly have it." The man gazed at the stone in wonder. It was a diamond, probably the largest diamond in the whole world, for it was as large as a person's head. He took the diamond and walked away. All night he tossed about in bed, unable to sleep. Next day at the crack of dawn he woke the wise man and said, "Give me the wealth that makes it possible for you to give this diamond away so easily."

In Conclusion

This book is about loving life, living life to the full, which is achieved through greater understanding, especially understanding the ageing process as we live our lives from the fifties onwards. We do not fall in love with what we do not know so any new understanding that has been gained will hopefully open the reader to see the years ahead as a time of endless possibilities for personal enrichment and fulfilment. If the door has been opened a bit further to enable you to face the challenge of living life with greater zest and hope, it will have been worthwhile.

Other Books by the Author

- *Who Cares? A Guide for All Who Care for Others,*
  COLUMBA PRESS, 1995

- *Falling in Love with Life, An Understanding of Ageing,*
  COLUMBA PRESS, 1996

- *Shekina Sculpture Garden,*
  GOVERNMENT PUBLICATIONS, 1997

- *Time-Out in Shekina, The Value of symbols in our Search for Meaning,* ELEONA BOOKS, 1998

- *Diary of a Hippy, Journeying Through Surgery,*
  ELEONA BOOKS, 2001

- *Saying Yes to Life, A Way to Wisdom,* ELEONA BOOKS, 2002

- *New Paths towards the Sacred, Awakening the Awe Experience in Everyday Living,* PAULIST PRESS, USA, 2008

- *In Gratitude, The Story of a Gift-filled Life,*
  ORPEN PRESS, 2015

- *My Indian Journal, Exploring Interfaith Connections,*
  ISPCK, INDIA, 2015

- *Shekina Exhibition Catalogue,*
  GOVERNMENT PUBLICATIONS, 2017

Titles related to *Love Life*

Surprised by Fire

Martina Lehane Sheehan

(CURRACH PRESS, €14.99) ISBN: 9781856076951

In this book, the author takes us into the sacred shrine that waits, invisibly, to be discovered in all human experiences. Telling us that now we are no longer victims, the author gives us glimpses of the enchanted place we one day hope to inhabit.

The author's sincere and life-long commitment to the spiritual quest together with her professional work and research into the issues she discusses, are all impressively gathered into these few pages.

Cancer, A Circle of Seasons

Anne Alcock

(CURRACH PRESS, €14.99) ISBN: 9781856077354

What do you do when life hits you a sucker punch, such as a cancer diagnosis? Do you talk? Do you journal? Do you pray? When the author was diagnosed with breast cancer, she did all of those things. This book is her way of helping anyone to reflect creatively about their life experiences. On anything. Not just illness...

This book includes prayers, diary entries and journaling questions for the reader.

All royalties will be divided between the Irish Cancer Society and Kerry Cancer Bus.

All books are available to order directly from www.currach.ie

THIS IS NOT THE END

Get the latest from your favourite author, including interviews, videos, articles, competitions and opportunities to tell us just what you thought about our latest releases.

Subscribe to our newsletter at

www.currach.ie

Follow us on Twitter, Instagram or find us on Facebook.

@CurrachPress

CURRACH
PRESS